מסורה

ArtScroll Series®

Rabbi Nosson Scherman / Rabbi Meir Zlotowitz
General Editors

REB
SIMCHA

Published by

Mesorah Publications, ltd

in conjunction with
yeshiva ohr elchanan
Jerusalem

SPEAKS

RABBI SIMCHA WASSERMAN'S
*insights and teachings on vital principles
of life and faith*

by
Yaakov Branfman
and Akiva Tatz

FIRST EDITION
First Impression . . . September 1994

Published and Distributed by
MESORAH PUBLICATIONS, Ltd.
4401 Second Avenue
Brooklyn, New York 11232

Distributed in Europe by
J. LEHMANN HEBREW BOOKSELLERS
20 Cambridge Terrace
Gateshead, Tyne and Wear
England NE8 1RP

Distributed in Israel by
SIFRIATI / A. GITLER—BOOKS
4 Bilu Street
P.O.B. 14075
Tel Aviv 61140

Distributed in Australia & New Zealand by
GOLD'S BOOK & GIFT CO.
36 William Street
Balaclava 3183, Vic., Australia

Distributed in South Africa by
KOLLEL BOOKSHOP
22 Muller Street
Yeoville 2198, Johannesburg, South Africa

Typography by Compuscribe at ArtScroll Studios, Ltd.

Printed in the United States of America by Noble Book Press
Bound by Sefercraft, Quality Bookbinders, Ltd. Brooklyn, N.Y.

This volume is a tribute to the
unforgettable gadol whose
teachings it presents

Rabbi Simcha Wasserman זצ״ל

הרה״ג ר׳ אלעזר שמחה

בן הרה״ג ר׳ אלחנן בונם זצוקלה״ה הי״ד

נפטר ב׳ מרחשון תשנ״ג

and to the woman who matched his idealism
and was his partner in accomplishment

מרת פיגא רחל בת הרה״ג ר׳ מאיר ע״ה

נפטרה י״ב מרחשון תשנ״ג

Few people so combined greatness with humility,
loftiness with accessibility, profound wisdom with
the ability to relate to anyone whatever his level.

They touched countless thousands; no one will
ever know fully how much better our world is
because of them.

Reb Simcha was our teacher, mentor,
spiritual father. Like so many others, we
pray that his influence will inspire our families
throughout the generations.

Barry and Bonnie Septimus

Gedalia and Rachael Weinberger

It is still too soon for us to think in the past tense of
Reb Simcha, our Rebbe, our mentor, our inspiration, our
support system and our "friend" b'lev v'nefesh. How can there
be a world without his presence? Who will exemplify the joy of
correct living? How masterfully he used sound relationships as
his springboard for personal fulfillment in the truest sense:
doing Hashem's work. As accomplished as Reb Simcha was in
hiding his amazing attributes, that's how demonstrative he was
in develping firm and lasting relationships, as with his adored
wife, students, colleagues and friends. He used these relationships openly, as conduits to ensure his success in teaching,
influencing and supporting every soul who touched him.

We appreciate the opportunity to dedicate this cherished
compilation of but a fraction of Reb Simcha's prolific
scholarship and insight in loving memory of our parents:

Mr. and Mrs. David Eisner
Dovid Yitzchok ben Yehoshua Dov
Chaya Golde bas Aaron

Mr. and Mrs. Sam Abramowitz
Shlomo Yitzchok ben Yosef Dovid
Malkah bas Yechiel

May all their generations reflect Reb Simcha's influence

Dr. and Mrs. Leo Eisner

In memory of

Hagaon Rabbi Simcha

Wasserman זצ״ל

and

Rebbetzin Faiga Wasserman ע״ה

Alice and Sidney Eisenshtat

Los Angeles, California

In loving memory of

Rabbi and Rebbetzin
Wasserman זצ״ל

Isadore and Lillian Levin

Dr. William and Linda Levin

Dr. Samuel and Diana Hirt

Los Angeles, California

In honor of

Isadore and Lillian Levin

for their lifelong dedication to

Yeshiva Ohr Elchanan

Morey A. Moore

In memory of

Hagaon Rabbi Simcha and Reb. Faiga Wasserman זצ״ל

and

Aaron Fuchs ע״ה

Simon and Hinda Manela ע״ה

By a Talmid

Rabbi Zalman Manela

Los Angeles, California

Dedicated in memory of
My Grandfather

Reb Dovid Schlussel זצ"ל
Rosh Bais Din of Munkacs
נפטר כ"ד אדר ת"יש

and his two sons
My Father

Reb Chaim Yechezkel ע"ה
נפטר י"ב אדר שני תשכ"ב

and My Uncle

Reb Noto Shlomo הי"ד
Perished in Auschwitz the week of Shavuos 1944

תהא נשמתם צרורה בצרור החיים

Akiva E. Schlussel
Los Angeles

לזכר נשמת

ר' פייבל לייב בן אליהו הלוי ז"ל

#ביילא בת יצחק ע"ה

Dedicated in their memory

by their children

David and Rivka Bass

and their sons

Yitzchak and Shaya

In memory of

Hagaon Rabbi Simcha Wasserman זצ"ל

and

Rebbetzin Faiga Wasserman ע"ה

Mr. and Mrs. Allen Jaffe
Valley Center, California

❧❦❧

In memory of

Hagaon Rabbi Simcha Wasserman זצ"ל

and

Rebbetzin Faiga Wasserman ע"ה

Sandy and Max Candiotty
Los Angeles, California

❧❦❧

In memory of

Hagaon Rabbi Simcha Wasserman זצ"ל

and

Rebbetzin Faiga Wasserman ע"ה

Dolores and Joe Simon
Beverly Hills, California

❧❦❧

Dedicated to the memory of
our beloved parents

Rabbi Yechiel Ephraim Fischel זצ"ל
and **Esther** ע"ה
Erster

Rabbi Chaim and Rose Feifer
Rabbi Moshe Yosef and Lillian Bobrowsky
Rabbi Shlomo and Edith Hochler
Rabbi Shneur and Phyllis Weinberg
Rabbi Avraham Yankel and Frances Gluckowsky

In Memory of

Hagaon Rabbi Simcha Wasserman זצ״ל

and

Rebbetzin Faiga Wasserman ע״ה

Pauline Roberts

Los Angeles, California

In honor of the
friends and supporters
of Yeshiva Ohr Elchanan who
help continue the mission
Reb Simcha began.

**Yeshiva Ohr Elchanan
Jerusalem**

Rabbi Moshe M. Chadash
Rosh HaYeshiva

מאור ירושלים

משותף של מרן Founded by:
רבי מאיר חדש זצ"ל Rav Meir Chadash זצ"ל
רבי שמחה וסרמן זצ"ל Rav Simcha Wasserman זצ"ל

Rav Moshe M. Chadash
Rosh HaYeshiva

בס"ד

ישיבת אור אלחנן
YESHIVA OHR ELCHANAN

ע"ש הגאון הקדוש
רבי אלחנן וסרמן הי"ד

Rav Elchanan
Wasserman הי"ד

סיון תשנ"ד

The publication of this book is a most significant and moving event for myself and for Yeshivat Ohr Elchanan. The book was begun while Rabbi Wasserman *z'tzl* was yet alive; it had his full support and encouragement, and the Yeshiva now has the honor of bringing it to fruition.

אדם חייב לומר בלשון רבו... (עדיות פרק א, משנה ג)

The authors have succeeded in capturing not only much of Rabbi Wasserman's Torah teaching, they have also captured the flavor of his words and his style. Anyone who had the merit to know the Rosh Yeshiva *z'tzl* will hear him speaking in these pages.

Rabbi Wasserman possessed a remarkable talent for speaking simply and yet with great depth; listeners on many levels of knowledge would find insight in his words intended for their particular level. He was also able to transmit deep Torah ideas to listeners who had no formal Torah background; therefore this book is suited both to the *talmid chacham* and also to the reader who is seeking an introduction to his heritage.

The authors are uniquely qualified for the task: R. Akiva Tatz is a cousin of the late Rosh Yeshiva, and was particularly close to him during Rabbi and Mrs Wasserman's years in Jerusalem. Rabbi Wasserman made it clear that he was the one to see this project through to its completion. R. Yaakov Branfman knew Rabbi Wasserman during the last phase in Jerusalem, and conferred with the Rosh Yeshiva on questions concerning the book. Together they undertook the work of transcribing and compiling Rabbi Wasserman's spoken word, and rendering it into readable form; it is important to know that the finished product is as faithful as possible to Rabbi Wasserman's own words.

It is a privilege for the Yeshiva, which Rabbi Wasserman himself founded and nurtured, to have published this volume of his teachings. I am certain that it will benefit those involved in Torah learning and teaching, and the entire Jewish world.

Rabbi Moshe Chadash
Rosh Yeshiva

רחוב אהליאב 27 ירושלים. ת.ד. 5662. טל. 583666   27 OHOLIAV ST., P.O.B. 5662, JERUSALEM, TEL. 583666

Contents

৵§ Publisher's Preface

We first came to know Rabbi Simcha Wasserman זצ״ל when we published the biography of his illustrious father זצוקללה״ה. Reb Simcha read and re-read the manuscript, commenting and correcting with the wisdom, good taste, and sense of history — past and future — that were uniquely his. As he always did, he tried to give the impression that he was a relatively ordinary son of a great father. He failed. It is true that he was able to mask his phenomenal knowledge of *Shas* from all but a few. Nevertheless, as one came to know him, to listen to his succinct and casual-sounding but profound comments on the Torah, on Jewish life, and on the needs and aspirations of individuals, one came to realize that one was in the presence of an extraordinary Torah personality — one who would have been just as outstanding if his name had not been Wasserman.

It is with particular pride, therefore, that we publish this collection of Reb Simcha's talks. We are especially pleased that the authors have captured not only his ideas, but his "voice." Those who knew him will read this book with pleasure and nostalgia, "seeing" him as they read, "hearing" the soft voice enunciating strong ideas that seemed tailor-made for his listeners, whether they were few or many. Those who did not know Reb Simcha will feel enriched by this book, because no one can read it without feeling that it speaks to him or her directly.

We are grateful to RABBI MOSHE CHADASH שליט״א, who joined Reb Simcha in founding and building Yeshivas Ohr Elchanan in Jerusalem, and who took the initiative in making this book a reality. Rabbi Chadash is a scion of an illustrious family, but he has earned his own reputation as a rosh yeshiva and dynamic force for Torah life. The yeshiva was Reb Simcha's main focus after he settled in Israel. He amazed us all with his vision and vitality as he traveled the world to enlist friends for the yeshiva, and he warmed everyone with his pride in the yeshiva's growth in size and stature. Under Rabbi Chadash's leadership, the yeshiva continues to thrive, and it remains the memorial to Reb Simcha's vision and dedication.

We are grateful to AKIVA TATZ and YAAKOV BRANFMAN, the authors, whose devotion to Reb Simcha is obvious in this volume; to ELI KROEN who designed the cover; to MRS. FAIGIE WEINBAUM and FAYGE SILVERMAN, who read and commented; and to MRS. BASSIE GUTMAN, DVORY GLATZER and CHAYA G. ZAIDMAN, who put the book into final form. SHMUEL BLITZ, director of ArtScroll Jerusalem, coordinated the trans-Atlantic production, assisted by RABBI AVROHOM BIDERMAN of our staff.

All Reb Simcha's life, he delivered the message of Torah, on three continents, in no way more eloquently than what he was and the way he lived. We pray that this book will help keep his legacy alive among those who knew him — and those who will make his acquaintance through these pages.

Rabbi Meir Zlotowitz
Rabbi Nosson Scherman

Tishrei 5755/September 1994

✑ Acknowledgments

We have attempted to convey Rabbi Wasserman's words as accurately as possible; however, some degree of collating and editing was necessary in order to present the material in written form. Any imperfections are our responsibility.

The following people provided invaluable assistance and we thank them:

RABBI MOSHE CHADASH sh'lita, Rosh Yeshiva of Yeshiva Ohr Elchanan and the yeshiva's co-founder with Rabbi Wasserman, who steered the production of this book from inception to completion; RABBI NOACH ORLOWEK sh'lita, well-known educator, author, and long-time talmid of Rabbi Wasserman, for careful checking of the manuscript and many essential additions and suggestions; R' AVRAHAM and ESTHER SUTTON, for important work with transcription of tapes, as well as all those who helped them; MRS. MINDE TATZ, for her customary meticulous work on the manuscript; R' YEHUDA LANDY, for expert assistance with references; MR. and MRS. ZVI SCHWARTZ for general assistance; the entire ArtScroll team — it has been a singular privilege to work with them on this Torah project; and our wives, whose assistance was essential every step of the way.

Y.B.
A.T.

Sivan, 5754
May, 1994

Biographical Notes

Yeshiva Ohr Elchanan/Jerusalem

The last great achievement of Reb Simcha ז״ל

Biographical Notes

This book is a record of some of Rabbi Simcha Wasserman's teachings, in his own words. It is not a biography — an adequate biography is a task which requires a book of its own. These introductory notes are intended to sketch, in broadest outline, the more than ninety years which Reb Simcha's life spanned, and the man who lived that life.

ELAZAR SIMCHA WASSERMAN was the oldest son of the great Rabbi Elchanan Wasserman *zt"l*, Rosh Yeshiva of the Baranovich **The Early Years** Yeshiva and a close *talmid* (student) of the Chafetz Chaim. The influence on Reb Simcha of his father and the other *gedolim* (great men) who were an essential part of his early years was to be life long. Eighty years later he would describe the experience of his first meeting with the

Chafetz Chaim and how deeply it had affected him, or what he had gained from being in the presence of his uncle, Rabbi Chaim Ozer Grodzensky, and of many of the Torah luminaries of that generation.

Rabbi Moshe Landinsky, in whose home he lived when he learned in Radin, Rabbi Chaim Soloveitchik, Rabbi Shimon Shkop, the Alter of Slobodka — these were some of the leaders of that generation with whom he was close.

Reb Simcha studied in the Novaradok Yeshiva for some years, beginning shortly after his *bar mitzvah*. Under the guidance of the Alter of Novaradok, he traveled from one place to another to teach students and to set up facilities for learning. In those days, which included the period immediately after the Russian Revolution, traveling was very dangerous. On one occasion he was caught without a travel permit (he was traveling to teach children) and sentenced to a work camp, cutting and transporting trees. During that period he was beaten by other prisoners. He awoke early every day to put on *tefillin* and *daven* (pray) before going out to work; and in order to adhere to the laws of *kashrus*, he ate only bread and water.

When Reb Simcha asked the commander for the day off on Shabbos, everyone laughed. But the commander gave it to him. He had seen how Reb Simcha was conducting himself and declared that he could see that the boy was sincere. The person who replaced him in the work crew was shot by a guard as a perverse punishment for the escape of another prisoner, and Reb Simcha later said that since he was the Jewish boy there, undoubtedly *he* would have been the one shot. He felt that Shabbos had saved his life.

When this ordeal was over and Reb Simcha was released, he was waiting to be taken across the border into Poland when he was arrested again by the Red Army and put in the custody of a commissar. When they were alone, the commissar revealed to Reb Simcha that he too was Jewish and released him. During the night he crossed the border, and after walking and crawling many kilometers, he entered Mezeritch. The Jews there took him in, and he stayed with a family over Shabbos. Reb Simcha later recalled his reaction when he saw his host change into Shabbos clothes: "I couldn't believe my eyes. Before going to *shul*, the man went to his closet, took out a Shabbos suit, and changed. I could not imagine that a man could have two suits. I came from Russia, a Communist country. There we had nothing. There was no fabric. I had a suit made from flour sacks. And he had a suit to change into! I couldn't believe it."

Eventually, via Brisk, he arrived in Baranovich, after being in jail, being beaten, and experiencing various other ordeals. "My mother came to fetch me and take me home. When my father came in and saw me, he made a *berachah* (blessing) *she'hecheyanu* and *mechayeh meisim*, opened a *gemara*, and said, 'Sit and learn.' "

During those difficult years he survived pogroms, on one occasion being left for dead in the street. He was in a hospital during one pogrom in which the Jewish patients were murdered. Reb Simcha happened to be in the infectious ward; the perpetrators were afraid to enter, and he survived.

❧ ❧ ❧

THE LAST TIME THAT Reb Simcha saw the Chafetz Chaim was immediately after the last Yom Kippur of the Chafetz Chaim's life,

Instructions from the Chafetz Chaim

and their meeting was particularly significant. He spent Yom Kippur in Radin and went in to say goodbye to the Chafetz Chaim the next day. As Reb Simcha was leaving, the Chafetz Chaim called him back and said, "You should know that when Mashiach comes, he's not going to forget anyone. Even if there is a single Jew at the other end of the world, Mashiach is not going to forget him."

Later, Reb Simcha would say of those parting words: "Somehow I felt that the Chafetz Chaim was giving me instructions. I knew then that I was going to be traveling."

From then on, he carried Radin with him wherever he went. He was always part of the community, and yet he was always a Jew of Radin.

Soon after that last visit to the Chafetz Chaim, the traveling began. His father sent him to Strasbourg, France, where he mastered French and established the only yeshiva existing in France at that time, which provided the seed for the flourishing Torah community existing there today. He remained there until 1938, when his father instructed him to begin teaching and spreading Torah in America.

This became a pattern: in a number of cities, he was the pioneer who walked into a wilderness devoid of Torah. He took it upon himself to do the hard work of digging wells that slowly started to bring forth the water of Torah learning and *Yiddishkeit*. When things were moving, he would leave the running of the institution to others, who were often hand-picked by him, and then quietly, unobtrusively, move on to another wilderness.

He established the first yeshiva in Washington Heights, the first full-time day school in Detroit, the first yeshiva in Los Angeles, and the first schooling for youngsters and adults in Southern California, which later provided the seed from which full-time day schools could spring forth there.

❀ ❀ ❀

DURING HIS FIRST YEARS IN AMERICA, he taught in Mesivta Torah Vodaath and became close to Reb Shraga Feivel Mendlowitz *zt"l*. The situation of the Jewish community, from a Torah viewpoint, was extremely low at that time. There was very little learning of Torah and very little Torah-true leadership. In 1941, Reb Mendlowitz decided to buy an estate in Monsey near New York and use it as a retreat to train a number of his students to take responsibility for the Jewish community in America. He asked Reb Simcha to come with him and to take charge of their Talmudic studies. They spent the summer months in Monsey, preparing themselves for leadership; the name of the program was *"Aish Dos."*

Teaching in America

In addition to their Torah studies, they would develop means for helping the community. Almost everyone who was there decided to go into education, fired with the ideal that they had to do something to raise the community to a knowledgeable level. Reb Simcha gave *gemara shiurim* (Talmudic lectures) and also taught those subjects which educators would need in order to be able to make real contributions to *kehillos* (communities) in America. The members of this group became the first principals and educators in yeshivos in places where it was previously thought impossible to establish genuine learning. They were in the front lines of a new organization that Rav Mendlowitz founded,

Torah Umesorah, which began setting up day schools across the United States.

WHEN THE WAR IN EUROPE broke out, representatives of the yeshivos joined to work for the benefit of all those who were in danger in Europe. The new organization was the Vaad Hatzalah; Reb Simcha was instrumental in its establishment and work.

During and After the War

As it became clear that a holocaust had started, he worked closely with Rav Aharon Kotler *zt"l*, feverishly devising and implementing a program to convince members of the Congress to pressure the U.S. government into taking some action. After several months of work, the project abruptly ended. "Some politicians, who felt their influence in Washington was necessary for other things, destroyed the project," explained Reb Simcha. They were forced to find other means to continue their work.

Soon after the end of the war, he volunteered to go to Europe, under the auspices of the Vaad Hatzalah. He worked in London, Warsaw, Prague, and Paris on behalf of the refugees. Characteristically, as soon as he accompanied a train of 400 orphaned children — collected from monasteries and convents — into Paris and later Aix-les-Bains, he organized yeshiva *bachurim* (young men) to come to Paris to learn with the children.

❦   ❦   ❦

REBBETZIN FEIGE RACHEL WASSERMAN was his partner in all his work. During his first two years in Los Angeles, she stayed behind in Detroit, where she was teaching, in order to send her salary to him so that he should be able to build Torah in California. On one occasion, he considered leaving Los Angeles in order to end their long separation. The Rebbetzin responded: "If *HaKadosh Baruch Hu* (the Holy One) has not given us children, it is for the sake of what you are doing. What else will we leave over? So I insist that you continue until you influence people and educate them as you must. That way many *yaldei Yisrael* (Jewish children) will be our children."

The Rebbetzin

THE ENERGY DID NOT LESSEN in his old age. In 1979, Reb Simcha and his Rebbetzin were finally able to fulfill their dream of

Israel and Ohr Elchanan

living in *Eretz Yisrael*. He immediately set to work on the project that would occupy the majority of his time and energy for the rest of his life: the establishment of a Torah center and a major institution of learning at the highest level. Together with Rabbi Moshe Chadash *sh'lita*, he established the yeshiva Ohr Elchanan in Jerusalem. Reb Simcha considered the yeshiva to be most closely following in the ways of his father. He poured into it the wisdom and experience gained during the decades he had spent raising *talmidim* (students) and building institutions of learning prior to his arrival in *Eretz Yisrael*.

The demands for admission increased to the point where the yeshiva outgrew its facilities. Close to the age of ninety, Reb Simcha took it upon himself to generate the major means of support for a new building in the Romema section of Jerusalem; he intensified his already taxing schedule of international travel. The yeshiva moved into the new building in early 1992. He also actively participated in the foundation of the new branch of the yeshiva in Tiberias.

RABBI WASSERMAN WAS a central figure in the *baal teshuvah* movement (movement of those who have a newly awakened interest in Torah Judaism); he had seen signs of its imminence before it became established, and he began to sensitize and prepare the Torah world for its role in fostering that movement. The movement had begun to bloom during the time he was living in Los Angeles, and the Wassermans had opened their yeshiva, their home, and their hearts to the new generation. After the move to *Eretz Yisrael*, they continued this special attention to *baalei teshuvah*. On Shabbos, their table overflowed with guests new to Torah, and Reb Simcha would regularly conduct question-and-answer sessions at the various *baal teshuvah* yeshivos in Jerusalem; much of the material in this book is drawn from those sessions.

Role in the Teshuvah Movement

REB SIMCHA PASSED AWAY late in 1992. The Rebbetzin sat *shivah* (seven-day mourning period) for him and spent the next Shabbos in the yeshiva. On *motzaei Shabbos* (Saturday evening) she fell ill, and the next morning she, too, departed this world. One of her last acts was to call Rabbi Moshe Chadash on that Friday as she arose from *shivah*, and to ask of him, as the Rosh Yeshiva of Ohr Elchanan, to continue her late husband's work of building the yeshiva as intensively as possible.

They Were Not Parted . . .

☙ ☙ ☙

AN ATTEMPT TO DESCRIBE Reb Simcha himself, the man, the personality, must await a full biography. But for the reader who never had the privilege of knowing him, these are the words of Rabbi Nachman Bulman *sh'lita:* "He was endless in his energies. Until the very last few months, his energy was that of a young man. The firmness in his step, his eyes, his face: it was not that of a ninety-year-old man. And more important, the smile in the eyes. It is not replaceable. That was the product of a factory whose head was Reb Elchanan, and whose head over the head was the Chafetz Chaim and the Torah community of the great yeshivos of Europe, and his connections with *gedolim* from every sector.

Beneath the Surface

"There was about him a feeling that a person who has that kind of energy until his very old age had to be a *tahor eynaim* (pure of eyes) and a *tahor lev* (pure of heart), and that he was *tahor* (pure) in every way. There was always such a feeling about him."

Reb Simcha dealt with his students as if they were his children. In his will he wrote that he forbade any *hespedim* (eulogies) at his funeral, unless his Rebbetzin were present, in which case he would permit just one *maspid* (eulogizer) to say just one *hesped*, and to say simply that he had attempted to teach each *talmid* according to his particular needs.

HE WAS SKILLED AT HIDING his greatness in learning and in character; one could easily have missed recognizing these unless one spent much time in his presence, when occasional opportunities afforded a glimpse beneath the unassuming and very approachable exterior.

The Art of Concealment

His way was to hide his own achievements and to focus on the greatness of Torah and service of Hashem. He asked very little for himself and was more concerned with giving of himself to others so that they might develop the potential greatness which he saw in each person.

Rabbi Chadash talked about Reb Simcha's great art of self-effacement. "He was a master at hiding himself. I was familiar with many of the sides of his personality; still, there were aspects that were revealed to me only after years of being close to him, during the last times that we were together. There were moments when I would suddenly see something new that would reveal another aspect of his greatness.

"Sometimes, when he was asked about something in learning, he would appear not to know exactly. 'Maybe it's like this, or maybe like this.' Afterwards, if someone would press him, 'You don't remember?,' the Rosh Yeshiva would start to talk with him, and in the course of the discussion he would gently give it over with many of the commentaries, which he knew by heart.

"Once we were in a certain city. He was invited to give a *shiur* (Torah lecture). He felt it would be good for our yeshiva, so he agreed. Before the *shiur*, we were together and there was some extra time, so he discussed the content of the *shiur* with me. There is an important discussion by Reb Chaim Brisker on that topic. We had some time, so we learned it and discussed it in depth. He wasn't planning on bringing it up in the *shiur*, but we went into it anyway. During the *shiur*, the Rabbi of the city interrupted and said somewhat sharply, 'Rav Chaim Brisker talked about this!' It was just what we had learned prior to the *shiur*; certainly, the Rosh Yeshiva hadn't forgotten. But he turned to the side, as one who is a little embarrassed. Then he continued. Everyone assumed, naturally enough, that he hadn't known that Reb Chaim had said that."

☙ ☙ ☙

HIS STUDENTS HAD THE FEELING that they were his equals and his closest friends. Every one of them felt that he was especially beloved — and each one was. Stories abound of Reb Simcha's ability to make friends with every person. ("You can't make someone be your friend, but you can be a friend to someone and hope they'll reciprocate.") Yet, somehow, there was the feeling about him that he was drawing on a reservoir that came from some other place and some other time

Friendships and Happiness

He always seemed to be happy; *"simcha"* means "joy." Even when discussing painful subjects, there was about him a relaxed equanimity. Once, during Pesach, one of the present authors had the privilege of having Rabbi and Mrs. Wasserman as guests. On that occasion, during one of the meals, we found one of the rare opportunities to ask about some of their personal experiences. Rabbi Wasserman described some of the harrowing events which had befallen him and his family during the torturous years following the First World War, including pogroms and other horrors. But the thing which struck us most was the gentleness of his voice and the softness of his tone. He could have been talking about matters entirely impersonal and unemotional. At one point, the Rebbetzin sighed deeply at the mention of family lost; Rabbi Wasserman turned to her, and in Yiddish softly said, "Feigele, we don't complain." Entirely calm and not put out in the least, Rebbetzin Wasserman replied, "I'm not complaining." And they continued answering our questions, smiling and at peace. It was, after all, Yom Tov.

When a student asked Rabbi Wasserman how he managed to maintain his remarkably calm demeanor so consistently, Rabbi Wasserman answered, "Long ago I made a decision to conduct

myself in a certain way: whenever I find myself in a situation which requires action, I do whatever I can; but if there is nothing I can do about a particular problem or situation, I do not worry about it at all."

❧   ❧   ❧

RAV CHADASH TALKS ABOUT the times that Reb Simcha spent Shabbos or Yom Tov together with the students in the **In Ohr Elchanan** yeshiva. "The Yamim Tovim were beautiful when he was there! He was living among us, eating with the *bachurim* on Shabbos or Rosh Hashanah night, sometimes giving *shiurim*. How much that added! It was a completely different atmosphere. There was nothing else like it.

"Although he gave us the most special experience in those times, he was very careful not to benefit in any way from the yeshiva. All his self-sacrifice on behalf of the yeshiva was in order to provide a place for students to learn, and to do this in memory of his father.

"In the beginning, he would attempt to pay me after Yom Tov for the food he had eaten. I said, 'Impossible! How can I take payment from you? You came for us.' Still, he wanted to pay for his food. He didn't want to accept my refusal.

"From then on, after Shabbos or Yom Tov, he would give me money and state that it was payment for an *aliyah* to the Torah that he had received, or a sum promised during *yizkor* (memorial service). It was a *neder* (oath). I wasn't able to refuse!"

⚜   ⚜   ⚜

REB SIMCHA'S TORAH and *chachmas ha'chaim* (life-wisdom) provided the solution to a difficult situation on many occasions.

Life-Wisdom Once, in California, the school inspectors tried to close down Reb Simcha's school. The reason was that the students spent all morning on their Torah studies and began studying the secular subjects only in the afternoon; the authorities were concerned that the students would be fatigued by then and unable to concentrate well. They felt that such an arrangement deprived the students of the opportunity to achieve adequately in their secular work. It was a tense moment; much of what Reb Simcha had built was being threatened.

He answered the authorities as follows: "If I teach secular subjects in the morning, I will not find good teachers because all the best teachers are already employed in the regular schools — the only teachers available are those who cannot find work. However, if I teach secular subjects in the afternoon, I can employ the best teachers since that is when they are free! I therefore arrange the school day in this way, and my students get the very best of secular teaching." The school was allowed to continue with no further problems from the secular authorities.

This solution was typical of Reb Simcha's genius: the perfect answer, and of course, perfectly true.

Just as Reb Simcha had the correct answers for all situations, he was also capable of a sharp answer when the occasion demanded. At a *sheva brachos* (post-wedding celebration) in California, hosted by a family belonging to a certain group of Chassidim, he was seated next to a rabbi from a non-Orthodox Jewish movement. The man addressed Reb Simcha: "Rabbi Wasserman, what are you doing here? I thought you disapproved of this particular Chassidic group!"

Replied Reb Simcha, "Not at all. An army has various parts — an Air Force, a Navy, infantry, and so on. Each has its own task and methods, but all are necessary for the army to function. These Chassidim are one part of the army of the Jewish people."

The man then asked, referring to his own non-Torah ideology, "And what part of the army are we?"

Without hesitation Reb Simcha replied, "You are the deserters!"

❧ ❧ ❧

HE WAS A MAN OF PEACE. He would quote the statement of the Sages to the effect that the only vessel capable of holding blessing is

Consideration and Concern

peace, and he lived it. In Los Angeles a certain individual conducted a personal vendetta against him; Rabbi Wasserman never replied to any of the accusations with which he was insulted. He later explained, "It takes two to make a *machlokes* (fight). If one does not respond, there can be no *machlokes*."

His gentleness and kindliness were palpable. In the street, he would not walk ahead of an elderly person whose pace was slow in case that person would feel his age more by seeing others walk faster. Once, while on his way to a function where he was to be the guest of honor, an old man recognized him and began reminiscing about days gone by. Although the man rambled on seemingly inter-minably, Rabbi Wasserman would not cut him short; instead, he listened patiently and attentively, with not the slightest sign of condescension or impatience. When he was finally on his way again, he said apologetically to those escorting him, "What could I do?"

❦ ❦ ❦

FOR US, RABBI WASSERMAN WAS a link with the previous generation of Europe. His personal account of his contact with the greats of that generation, in particular his father Reb Elchanan and the Chafetz Chaim, gave us the feeling that we were somehow part of that world. He would tell us things he had learned from his father. An example:

Bridge From the Past

"Once, my father *zt"l* had to travel from Baranovich and I was accompanying him to the station; we were walking together and I was carrying his small suitcase. He was wearing new boots that my mother had bought for him, which he had refused to wear until my mother gave away his very old and worn shoes to the girl who carried the water buckets through the snow, explaining to my father that the girl had no shoes and therefore needed them. Only then had he agreed to wear the new ones. I could see that something was bothering him. After a while he said, 'These boots are bothering me.' My father never spoke without a specific reason, so I knew that I was about to learn something. 'What is bothering me is that they have laces, and I reckon that it is going to cost me half a minute a day to tie and untie them.' He was teaching me the value of time."

REB SIMCHA HAD THAT deeper perception which accompanies Torah greatness. On one occasion, one of us went to him to ask a question about a complex and difficult life situation. A number of people and variables were involved in the problem, so it was necessary to preface the question with a lengthy introduction presenting all the relevant facts. During the first sentence of this introduction, Rabbi Wasserman quietly said, "Your question is . . .," and proceeded to state the question accurately, and answered it immediately.

Deeper Knowledge

On another occasion, two of us were learning with Rabbi Wasserman at his home in Jerusalem; we had the privilege of such learning sessions with him weekly. A few days earlier, the two of us had privately begun studying a certain subject which is not commonly studied. Rabbi Wasserman looked across the table, emphatically stated the name of that subject, and proceeded to give us an exhaustive lecture on the correct approach to it. Some time later, the two of us began the private study of a particular *sefer* (book), which happens to be very rare and is almost unknown. Within days, at our weekly session with Rabbi Wasserman, he looked at us with a strange expression, stated the name of that *sefer*, proceeded to tell us what his father and the Chafetz Chaim had said about its author, and gave us guidelines concerning its study. Needless to say, we remained silent; what was there to say?

❧ ❧ ❧

REB SIMCHA EXPLAINED the *gemara* (*Kesuvos* 17a) which says that when the *Chachamim* (Sages) ordained the great Rav Zeira,

Unadorned Beauty

they sang these words: "*Lo k'chol, v'lo s'rak, v'lo pirchus; v'yaalas chen*," meaning that he does not adorn himself in any way but is very beautiful. The idea, Reb Simcha said, is not that Rav Zeira had beauty and refinement even though he did not adorn himself; but rather, *because* he did not adorn himself, he had the true, original beauty and refinement.

Rav Chadash adds, "The *gemara* is saying that this is how a Rav should be. No exaggeration. No self-inflation. Humility. Simplicity. Clearly the *gemara* is talking about the Rosh Yeshiva zt"l."

REB SIMCHA
SPEAKS

Reb Simcha Speaks

The room is crowded. Those present include rank beginners and accomplished scholars. Some of the beginners are attending their first Torah lecture ever. They have all come to hear the master educator and Rosh Yeshiva, who, besides being one of the leading Talmudic scholars of the generation, is known for his genius in the field of transmitting Torah to the uninitiated. His gift is the ability to convey the deepest Torah ideas in terms of first principles; the listener needs no formal background in Jewish learning at all — only an open mind, unclouded logic, and the desire to grow.

Their attention is riveted on the speaker. His grey-blue eyes radiate an indescribable warmth. Decades of immersion in Torah and life's intensity are distilled in those eyes; a lifetime bridging the Torah greatness of Europe, the hell of its destruction, and the modern era. The voice is clear; that it speaks personally to each one present is not in doubt. The face is rich with wisdom and a simple clarity. There is a timeless quality that invests the man, and a quiet but palpable joy. It is hard to remember that he is well over ninety.

Someone asks a question, and Rabbi Wasserman begins speaking.

The Marvel of Teshuvah —
The Return To Jewish Values

DAYBREAK

I saw something once as a young man which has remained with me. It was in Telz, which is very far north in Lithuania, where the summer nights are extremely short. One motzaei Shabbos we made havdalah around midnight, and a few of us took a walk out of town. Telz is not a big city, and soon we were in the fields where there were no street lights. Then I saw the sunset and the sunrise at the same time. The northern sky was dark; in the east the sky was already pale with the dawn, while the western sky was still red from sunset.

Much later in life I realized that what I had seen then was a mashal, an allegory, for this generation. We saw the sunset of a generation of Torah life in Europe; we have lived through the night which followed. And now we see dawn breaking, a new generation of Torah life and learning beginning.

This seems to be a pattern in Jewish history. There are prophecies that after times of darkness for the Jewish people, there will be times of daybreak and bright light. We go through a tragedy — dark times — and we come out reinforced. We are witnessing that right now. Many people who have been driven in one direction all their lives are stopping and beginning to think, "Which way are we going?" They are trying to think about it seriously. I never before saw this phenomenon happening on such a large scale. You cannot compare conditions in the Jewish world now with the way they were twenty-five years ago. We are actually witnessing daybreak.

PROPHECIES FOR OUR TIMES

In 1913, the Chafetz Chaim talked of history as a turning wheel which was about to start spinning faster and faster. Before the First World War, which ushered in the era of massive changes to the global map, he pointed out that international changes which had formerly taken centuries to occur would now take place in months. This has been happening continually since that time. He said that the reason was because we were coming close to the time of Mashiach, and many accounts would need to be adjusted speedily.

In Chumash *Devarim* (Deuteronomy), there are things written which are coming to pass now. There it is written that after we become old in the land — not fresh anymore — we shall begin to be disloyal to Hashem. We shall be exiled from the land and dispersed among the nations, where we shall remain in small numbers and continue to sin. Then we shall search sincerely for Hashem and we shall find Him. After we experience troubles and tribulations, at the end of days we shall return to Hashem and listen to His voice. He will not let us perish.

In the Torah portion of *Nitzavim*, this idea is repeated, and it says that we shall return, and our children will return, and Hashem will bring us back from among all the nations where we are dispersed.

We live in a very unusual time. So many people who have so little Jewish information in their backgrounds are turning to Torah. The Almighty Himself is bringing back people who were lost. He Himself has prepared this generation. Yechezkel (Ezekiel) the Prophet talks about this. He says in chapter 34, "...And they were scattered, because there was no shepherd, and they became food for all the animals of the field..." Then he says, in the name of the Almighty, "...I will seek that which was lost and bring back those who strayed. I will bandage the injured, and I will strengthen the sick..."

🍃 *Teshuvah* means that we come back to Hashem, and the period of Mashiach is the period when Hashem comes back to us. After all our experiences with exile, we are in a time of *teshuvah*, of people returning to Hashem, as was prophesied. Through this, Hashem is returning to us and will usher in the period of Mashiach. We have the very strong feeling that we are part of the generation that Hashem is bringing back to Himself.

The Almighty has said, through the prophet Malachi, "I will send you the prophet Eliyahu (Elijah) ahead of the great and fearful day of Hashem," and He goes on to say, "He will bring back the heart of parents to children." Rashi explains, "He will bring back the heart of the parents to the Master of the World, *through* the children." The children will lead.

We feel that those who have returned are those whom Eliyahu has selected to lead the Jewish people to the redemption of Mashiach. There will be hundreds and thousands, and their numbers will grow faster and faster. Then the whole nation will be privileged to greet Mashiach.

THE ALMIGHTY SEARCHING FOR HIS PEOPLE

There is a little park as you come into the religious neighborhood of Ezras Torah in Jerusalem. You can go there sometimes and it looks like it's full of flowers . . . It's all children! They're filling the entire park like flowers. This is happening all over Jerusalem.

We have prophecies that have already been realized: "Foxes will walk on the site of the Kodesh Kadashim (Holy of Holies)," referring to the destruction of the Temple. There are other prophecies that will also be realized. The prophet Zechariah says that people will sit in Jerusalem and rejoice. Then he says, "The streets of the city of Jerusalem will be filled with children playing." We see that blessing already. So I know that the other prophecies will also be realized. Hashem will rebuild Zion and Jerusalem.

There is a Torah-observant person who was head of the bacteriology department of a California university. On his office door he had a *mezuzah*. One day he was walking with a non-Jewish colleague who saw the *mezuzah* on the door and asked him what it was. As he was about to answer, he was called to the telephone. A non-Jewish student who was there took over and explained the whole idea of the *mezuzah* to the professor, in great detail, as if she were explaining from the textbook *Sefer HaChinuch*.

The Jewish professor couldn't understand how she knew so much about Jewish things. He knew that she came from a pious Catholic family in Mexico. He asked her, and she explained that for the past two years she had taken an interest in Judaism for no obvious reason and had read a lot.

When he told me the story, I told him that when he returned to the university, he should try to find out whether her family had a trace of Marranos in its history. It turned out that it did.

I had put the pieces together. I knew that many Marranos, Jewish escapees from the Inquisition who had pretended to convert to Catholicism but secretly continued to observe Judaism, had come to Mexico. I had heard that in some villages today in Mexico, there are women who go to the basement on Friday night and light candles, and they themselves don't know why they do this, except that it has been a family tradition for the past several hundred years. I remembered the prophecy from the prophet Yechezkel, which says that there will come a time when Hashem will bring back those who have been lost among the nations. I put this all together, and I thought that there was a good chance that she was a Marrano.

◦§ All this shows that there is a selection going on now. Some people are being brought back, and some people, due to the high intermarriage and assimilation rate, are being thrown out. There are also prophecies concerning that unfortunate fact. Those prophecies state that there will be members of the Jewish body who will be removed from it.

But to a large extent, there is something special happening at this point in history: a tremendous inspiration, an *impulse*. In the recent past it was not like this at all. A certain well-known news magazine came out with an article during those dark years, and entitled it

"The Vanishing Jew in America." It made the point that in America — in the whole world — as it was then, the Jew was vanishing. What happened was that the magazine vanished; it does not exist today. But we experience a revival, a renaissance, which is miraculous. This is in the category of wonders which we cannot explain — the wonders of our survival.

THE CALL

I heard something repeated in the name of the Radomsker Rebbe, in his *sefer* called *Tiferes Shlomo*. It says in the Torah portion *Vayechi* that when Yaakov Avinu was bidding farewell to his children, he said, "Come together, and I will tell you what is going to happen to you at the end of days." The spelling of one word in that sentence, *yikra*, which we translate as "what will happen to you," is very unusual. It should be spelled with the letter *hei* at the end. Instead, it is written with an *aleph* at the end, which changes the meaning from "happen" to "calling."

The *Tiferes Shlomo* talks about this, referring to the way in which one halachically takes possession of an article. The act of transferring possession from one person to another for portable things, or for animals, is called *kinyan meshichah*. This means that the act of acquisition occurs when the item is pulled by you — when you cause it to move. When dealing with animals, you can strike it with a stick and the animal moves, or else you make the animal move by calling it and it comes to you.

In terms of the relationship between Hashem and the Jewish people, the period of Mashiach can be considered the time when the Almighty finally takes full possession of His people. During all of our previous history, the Jewish people were often drawn closer to Hashem through being beaten with a stick, so to speak. From the time that we began to be prepared to receive the Torah, in *Mitzraim* (Egypt), we were given a certain preservative, which was not a very pleasant one, but which kept us from assimilating. The Master of the World turned the hearts of the Egyptians to hate His people. This was the Jewish people's blessing. This is what did not let them assimilate and what gave them the ability to develop as a people and to be ready for receiving the Torah.

In the Torah portion of *Vayigash*, we are told that when Yaakov Avinu was on his way to Egypt, he felt that the time in Egypt was going to be an unpleasant experience. He had a revelation in Beersheva, in which Hashem said to him, "Do not be afraid. I will go down together with you and I will bring you back." Sforno explains that Hashem was saying, "This is necessary in order to cement your children to become a nation. Here in Canaan where you are looked upon as equals, you do not yet have the Torah to protect you from assimilation, and you are therefore exposed to great danger. You have to go down to a place where the people — the Egyptians — by their laws cannot even sit together to eat with a Jew at one table. There you will be formed as a nation and will become ready to receive the Torah."

The oppression and persecution which often followed periods of assimilation in our history can be considered the way in which Hashem drew us closer to Him.

However, says the *Tiferes Shlomo*, the sentence in which Yaakov Avinu talks to his sons about the end of days refers to the second type of acquisition: the *calling*. The use of the *aleph* — "to call" — tells us that Yaakov Avinu is saying to his sons, "I will show you what will happen in the end of days. There will be a *call!* Hashem will just call us and we'll come." This is what the Master of the World is showing us in our days. This is what so many have experienced. We see it.

AWAKENING

In Paris recently, I was present at a *Yom haTorah* which took place throughout the entire country. Tens of thousands of people came that Sunday to the airport in Paris, where many aspects of Jewish life were demonstrated and explained. The Chief Rabbi of France proclaimed that the next Shabbos, every Shabbos-observant family should invite a non-Shabbos-observing family as guests. On the following day they had expositions at the airport: exhibits to explain a *bris milah* (circumcision), a *bar mitzvah*, a Jewish wedding, a kosher kitchen, laws of family purity. People demonstrated how they made meat kosher. Workshops and lessons in Torah took place in seminar rooms. The Sephardic Chief Rabbi came from Jerusalem and spoke in the main area. People came from all over France to learn about *Yiddishkeit*. There is a yeshiva there now. I lived in France in the past, when all this would have been completely impossible. But this is happening all over the world.

◄§ One day I attended a *bris* at nine o'clock in the morning. A little Jew had been born and was introduced to the nation. At ten o'clock, I was at a *cheder*. The teacher had learned the entire Torah portion of *Vayikra* with the children. They knew all the laws of the sacrifices: the *chattas*, the *asham*, and the *olah*. They were five and a half years old. All of the children in that class were children of *baal teshuvah* families. I was so impressed that I said to somebody near me, "If I were Mashiach, I would come right away." At one-thirty that day I attended another *bris*. At three-thirty I was talking to a beginners' class in one of the *baal teshuvah* yeshivos. Every one of these is a step in the rebuilding of the Jewish people. Hashem is rebuilding us right now.

The inspiration to *teshuvah* is affecting not only us. I heard that at Stanford University in California, the professor gave a lecture on evolution, and three-quarters of the class, mostly non-Jews, stood up and protested. This shows that there is some inspiration leading us away from atheism. The morning light and the daybreak are affecting the whole world. The sudden breakup of the Communist world is another example of this. There are many other unusual things occurring.

In one of the *haftarohs* which we read on Shabbos, it says, "I am the Almighty. When the time will come, I will hurry it up." The *gemara* says that this refers to the period of the redemption, of Mashiach.

In the Jewish world, the entire climate has changed. Things are happening very fast. Entire yeshivos are suddenly filled beyond capacity with people wanting to study, and the demand is not lessening. People from everywhere, sometimes without knowing why, pack up their suitcases and go to yeshivos or come to Jerusalem. Some of them stand at the Western Wall, and a man who is well known for this comes up to them and says, "*Shalom Aleichem.* Have you seen a yeshiva yet? Do you know what a yeshiva is? Come . . ." He takes them up the stairs near the Western Wall to a lecture, and many of them end up staying.

I talked to a young man in a yeshiva and asked him how he had arrived there. He told me that he had come to Israel to work in a kibbutz of the *Hashomer Hatzair* movement. They are the extreme leftists, almost Communist, and very anti-religious. During his time there, he was traveling and was in a taxi. On the seat he saw a magazine called *Shema Yisrael*, put out by one of the *baal teshuvah* yeshivos, which is a very sincere and beautiful publication. He asked the driver what it was, and the driver took a look and got angry. "I don't know. Most likely a passenger was here in the car and left it." The young man took the address, and the next morning he went to Jerusalem and he still hasn't gone back. He has been in yeshiva for a few years. There are many, many stories like this.

◄§ "When the time will come, I will hurry it up." Sometimes I travel, and I don't have time to prepare myself beforehand. Then I find that it's ten minutes before I have to go and I have not packed yet. So I open a suitcase, and I take an item from here and an item from there. I put it together, and I'm running as I do it. It's late and I'm in a rush. It seems that in the time before Mashiach's arrival, if the nation is not ready yet, He hurries us up. He has to hurry to prepare a generation to welcome Mashiach. So He throws people in His suitcase. There are more *baalei teshuvah* and more Torah students than before. There are more yeshivos in more places than before, and there is more learning everywhere. It's a beautiful thing. Hashem is packing His suitcase and is in a hurry to bring us into it.

In spite of that magazine's story, the Jewish people are not vanishing. We are coming back to life. This is a promise which was made to our mother Rachel. The prophet Yirmiyahu (Jeremiah) says, "Rachel cries for her children," and the answer is heard that "there is a reward … your children will come back to their boundaries." This refers both to physical boundaries and to spiritual boundaries. There has never been a time in our history when there was a movement of return like there is today. We are not afraid of Jewishness disappearing. But many individual Jews *are* disappearing. There are many issues connected with the role of the Torah-observant person in helping others to be aware of the inspiration and to "pack their suitcases."

Concerning the Torah it is written, "For this is your wisdom and your understanding in the eyes of the nations," because they will desire to be like you. This is the true kindness: to show and to lead others to the true path, like Avraham Avinu did. Many of our Sages talked about ways in which we can do this.

WHAT MAKES A JEW WANT TO BE A JEW?

The *gemara* says that Avraham was called "Avraham the Ivri" — "Avraham the Hebrew" — from the root word meaning to be "on the other side." The Sages say that the entire world is on one side and Avraham is on the other side, and he remains Avraham. So we have been told that perhaps the entire world will be against us, but it doesn't make us feel smaller and it does not change anything. It may definitely endanger us, as has happened before, and we hope it will not happen again. But it does not prevent the survival of the Jewish people.

When a Jew wants to be a non-Jew, then being a Jew is very hard. But if someone *wants* to be a Jew, it's not that hard. It's possible that there are some people who wish they were not born Jews. The motivations for this could be childish or they could be mature. A childish motivation, for example, might be that there is an exclusive golf club and it bothers them that they cannot get into it.

On the other hand, if a person knows that by being a Jew he has the whole world against him and he feels the opposition from all sides, then he may come to wish he had been born a non-Jew just so he should not feel threatened. We don't call this "correct," but it may not be a childish reaction. It may be very serious and very real. Some people in the concentration camps may have felt this way.

But it doesn't matter, because once you are born a Jew, nothing will help. So every Jew should want to be a Jew, because he is paying the price anyway. As long as he is paying the price, he should get the merchandise.

The question is: What makes a Jewish person want to be a Jew? The answer is: only Torah. This comes about not necessarily because of the conscious information that we learn. It comes about primarily through the subconscious influence that Torah has on a

Jewish person. There are parts of Torah that are very difficult to understand; however, the *real* force of Torah is not the taste of "chewing" it, of understanding it, but rather the influence you receive by taking it into your system. If you learn Torah correctly, it is a living thing. It penetrates your subconscious whether you know it or not. It has been designed to make a Jew out of a Jew. When the Torah was given, that's what it was given for: to make a Jew out of a Jew.

We know that wherever there is learning of Torah, there is inspiration, light, and continuation. There is only one kind of road sign guiding the Jewish person to return to the Creator and to His people, and that is the study of Torah. The words of the Almighty to the prophet Jeremiah are: "They have neglected Me and My Torah they have not guarded." Our Sages remark, "The Almighty says, 'I wish they would have guarded My Torah in study, even when they neglected Me in action. The inner light of Torah would have corrected them.' "

◄§ The Dubno Maggid quotes a *midrash* which talks about the verse "And it was night, and it was morning . . ." in the Torah portion of *Bereishis*. "It was night" refers to the activities of the wicked. "It was morning" refers to the activities of the righteous. Hashem says about the light, "It is good."

The Maggid says, "Do you need a *midrash* to tell you that the righteous — symbolized by the light — are preferred? No. It means something else. It is referring to the different ways in which people learn.

"A person can go to any school and see the failure of the larger society and decide not to be wicked because it leads to the collapse of society. Or a person can go to school in a society of *tzaddikim* (righteous people) and see the harmony within families, the happiness, the contentment. Which school does Hashem prefer? Clearly the latter, which is the yeshiva, the school of light."

◄§ Our Sages also say, as if quoting the Almighty, "I created the evil inclination, and I created Torah study to balance it." This indicates that Torah study is the only method which can succeed in directing the Jewish person to his goal and function. Strength for the life of Torah does not come from propaganda for Judaism. It comes enduringly only from the fullness of Torah learning. There is nothing which can sell Torah and *Yiddishkeit* to a person like Torah itself.

◦§ Whoever tries to be a salesperson for Torah is mistaken. One who tries to bring the Jewish people back to their fold by any other method is similar to a man trying to lift a load manually which can be handled only by a lifting machine — a crane. If a person would say, "Why should I bother with the machine? I'll lift it myself," it wouldn't move.

Hashem says that the mechanism which handles the evil inclination is the Torah. To move the evil inclination, there is no machinery other than Torah. If somebody tries to correct people, or to attract people, or to do a good salesman's job for Shabbos or for *kashrus*, he is trying to be a salesperson for Torah. It's like the one who is trying to lift the load by himself instead of using the crane. It doesn't work. To lift the load there is a machine, and you have to set the machine in motion and it will do it. Torah is called *Toras Chaim* — a Torah of Life. It has automatic drive, much like power steering, which just needs to be set in a certain direction, and the mechanism does all the work.

DRAWING OTHERS CLOSE

You cannot argue with people, because you always feel you are right and they always feel they are right. I have never seen that people came to a better understanding as the result of an argument. But if you learn with them, they'll see what you see, and then you don't have to explain it to them.

The Rambam says that the first step is to correct a person's character. The *gemara* says that if you have a student who doesn't behave correctly, don't push him away with both hands. Rather, push him with your left and pull him with your right. It's very interesting. If I simply push him away, I create a distance. But if I push with the left and pull with the right, I turn him. This means that you have to find the way to turn a person. Until you have turned him, you really haven't accomplished anything.

The Master of the World created the evil inclination, which prevents a person from turning. He also created the Torah, which enables a change in character to take place. There is an extraordinary relationship between the study of Torah and good behavior.

It is true, however, that there may be some people who are studying Torah and their character is nevertheless not very good. The Dubno Maggid talked about this, and he gave a parable:

> A salesman comes to a city with a sample case, which he has left at the train station. He comes to the hotel and calls over a boy and says to him, "I left my package at the station. Would you bring it for me? I'll pay you for it."
>
> The boys asks him, "Is it heavy? I'm a young boy and I can't carry a heavy load."
>
> "No, it weighs only three pounds."
>
> The boy goes to the station, and after an hour he's still not back. Finally after an hour and a half the door opens and the boy falls in, exhausted, sweaty, excited. He shows the salesman a big package and says, "Some nerve! Three pounds! It's all of sixty pounds! I *shlepped* it the whole way!"
>
> The salesman says, "Young man, are you sure that package weighs sixty pounds and not three pounds?"
>
> "Absolutely!"
>
> "Then, young man, you brought me the wrong package. *Shlep* it back! Bring me mine. If you became tired, it's not my fault, it's not my package."

The Dubno Maggid is saying that if you see that Torah has not straightened out the character, there is something wrong with the way that person is taking it in. It's not the right package. If it's the right package, it straightens out a person.

That is the idea of the power steering. If I want to influence a person in the correct way, *I* shouldn't do it. Like power steering, I have only to take the Torah and the Torah will do it. In the beginning we take a little piece of Chumash and we try to understand it, and little by little it penetrates. Just as someone who has fasted for forty years cannot be given a lot of food at one time, but must be fed tiny bits, similarly someone who has been spiritually starved for years has to be fed tiny bits.

I can't expect people to start keeping all the *halachos* (laws) of Shabbos right away. But on the other hand, we know that learning Torah without the intention of observing it is not *Toras Chaim*, a Torah of Life. It is not true Torah. Torah has to have the life force and vitality in it. In order for this to happen, it has to be learned according to the instructions of how Torah must be learned. One of those instructions consists of intending to live up to what we learn. Here we have a dilemma, because we are talking about people who do not, at the present time, intend to live up to what they learn. It's fine and pleasant, but the Torah that you learn with them loses all strength. It becomes a dead thing. It has no *neshamah* (soul) and provides no inspiration.

Therefore, in the beginning we learn things which do not require a commitment. We learn the stories in the beginning of the Chumash, like in the portion of *Lech Lecha*, about Avraham's travels from his homeland to *Eretz Yisrael*. In these stories there is nothing to be found which requires people to commit themselves. But it is Torah, and Torah has inspiration. Or we learn *Pirkei Avos* — Ethics of the Fathers. Sometimes, if we feel we can, we encourage a person to make a *berachah* on learning Torah before his learning that day, so that he realizes that he is really learning Torah, not simply nice stories.

When I first arrived in California, I taught many people this way. Many later asked me, after they were already keeping the *mitzvos* of the Torah, "How come you never told us to keep Shabbos, and how come we are keeping Shabbos?" I didn't do it. Torah did it. My job was to figure out which parts of Torah they could take. I selected parts of Torah which were true Torah. If I would have learned the laws of Shabbos with them, they would not have been able to accept it, because they were not ready to live up to it. But what I taught was genuine Torah, and it affected them.

> One day a young man came in and said to me, "I am about to become a father. I would like some advice."
> I said, "The first thing is to see that your child has a father."
> I explained this some more, and he said, "Do you mean that I should close my store on Shabbos?"
> I said, "Start learning."

Today that home is spiritually one of the most beautiful Jewish homes in his city. He says a *gemara shiur* on Shabbos, and his children are studying in yeshivos and are outstanding in their diligence. It started not by forcing him to keep Shabbos, but by telling him to start learning.

There were times when parents were angry with me because I brought their children close to Torah. It requires a lot of sensitivity in those cases. Sometimes a father is embarrassed if his child doesn't want to eat from his dishes. To him, it means that his child looks down on him. No father wants his child to look down on him. So it takes great sensitivity for the student to realize that the only difference between his father and him is that he was lucky enough to have the opportunity to see Torah, and that there is nothing wrong with his father.

The student has to learn that the fact that he ended up in a yeshiva is something wonderful that happened both to him and to his parents, and that one day his parents will unquestionably see how good it is.

◆§ People make the serious mistake of thinking that if their child comes close to Torah, he is estranged from them. It's just the opposite. The child acts with understanding and honor towards his parents, and the parents actually *find* their children that way. We don't have a generation gap. It's just the opposite.

RAMBAM'S GUIDELINES FOR
EDUCATING TO SPIRITUAL STRENGTH

If you see an article that someone has lost, the *halachah* is that you should not go away from it but should pick it up and endeavor to return it. While you have it in your possession, you are its guardian and are responsible for it. These are the laws of *hashavas aveidah*, returning lost items. This is a *mitzvah* and there are many guidelines for it.

Similarly, if a person has lost his most precious item, his Jewishness, it is my obligation to bring it to him. There are issues concerning the details of that obligation and how to carry it out. As with every other *mitzvah*, it has its guidelines and instructions concerning how it should be done.

The Rambam provides guidelines and insists that you should attract people to Torah with *divrei shalom* — "peaceful information." This means, in the Rambam's words, that "until they return to the strength of Torah," we should teach them things which do not require commitment. He explains that this is because to truly observe Torah requires spiritual strength.

The Rambam says that it is a very serious thing if a person does not recognize the authority of the Oral Torah. This is the extreme case of spiritual weakness, and it takes the person out of being considered part of the Jewish people. But then he says that this is only the case when the person himself originated his denial of Torah's authority. The children and grandchildren of those who veered away should be looked upon as having been forced into that situation. If they have not been raised and trained with Torah, you cannot criticize them for not living up to its standards. He goes even further and says that even if, later in life, they come into contact with Jewish communities where there are full Jewish standards and they are not diligent in adopting the standards of the community, don't blame them, because they were raised differently, and you cannot expect people in their adulthood to suddenly change their ways. He is saying that for many years they have seen other standards and have become part of those other standards. Don't expect them to jump and change. They were raised on those errors.

On the other hand, the Rambam says, *it is your duty to attract them to Torah with peaceful information*, information which does not force them to commit. One day they'll come to you. When the Torah gives them motivation to live a Torah life, then they have returned to the strength of Torah.

Arguments and attempts to persuade people do not work. Warm, gentle words may succeed. One should always remember the story about the sun and the wind: once, the sun and the wind had a competition to see who could strip a man of his coat. The wind tried first; it blew hard, but the man held firmly onto his coat. It blew a gale, but the man only clutched his coat more tightly. Then the sun tried: it shone warmly — and the man took off his coat himself.

EDUCATION FROM SAFE GROUND

In Ethics of the Fathers, the *Anshei Knesses HaGedolah* (Men of the Great Assembly) give over three central teachings, in which we can find advice about *kiruv* (drawing people closer to Torah).

The three things they state are: 1) Be slow to judge. 2) Raise many students. 3) Make a fence for the Torah.

Their first two principles teach how you are supposed to interact with the person you are being *m'karev* — drawing close. The third one is advice to the person who is doing the teaching. The idea of making a fence for the Torah means that someone who is in an environment where he is working to draw others close must make a fence for himself so that he should not be influenced by the surroundings.

The *Midrash* tells of a man who fell off a boat. The captain threw him a rope and said, "Hold on to the rope and it will keep you alive." It does not say that the captain jumped into the water. He remained where he was and threw the rope.

Working with others requires a great deal of sensitivity. We are part of society today, and yet we are strangers to it. We are an island. The person I am working with shouldn't feel that I am a stranger. He should feel that I am there with him, but I myself should not forget that I am a stranger to the society that he is still a part of. As much as I dwell with other people, I stand my ground and do not go to his ground. I throw the rope in and try to bring him to me, but I don't jump in. I stay on safe ground. I do not want to be drowned.

The *esrog* — citron — which we take on Succos is held apart from the other species. It has a good smell, and it has a good taste. Good character traits are compared to a good smell. Even if you are standing at a distance, you still get the good smell. Likewise, a person who has good character and a pleasant personality can be seen even from a distance. It's something you can feel. You don't have to come close, you just have to look at his face. He's a friend and you can feel it.

In addition, scholarship, of course, is very important. The *esrog* also has a good taste. Scholarship is compared to taste. You have to hear the wisdom — you have to eat the fruit — in order to appreciate it. The *esrog* symbolizes the scholar who has a pleasant personality. He is the ideal person.

The *hadassim* — the myrtle leaves — which we also take on Succos are mixed in with the other species. They have only a good smell. That represents good character without scholarship. This is very difficult, because more than good character is needed in order to teach; information must be transmitted in order to bring into effect the changes in the personality and character which are necessary to come to the strength of Torah.

The *lulav* — palm — which we take is from the date tree. It is also mixed in with the other species. The date is a very tasty fruit, but it has no aroma. This represents scholarship without character. There may be a scholar who is not loved by the people, but he may perform a function in keeping them together. But in terms of drawing people close, he may not have a function.

The last species we take on Succos are the *aravos*, the willow. It has no taste and no smell. It needs special care because it wilts in no time. *Content* preserves, but people who have no content cannot be preserved. A philosophy which has no content has no survival.

Thus, from the *esrog* which we take on Succos we learn that the ideal in education is to be a person who is *with* others, letting them taste the *emes* (truth), but also quietly standing apart, letting the best part of himself and his Torah radiate outward like a good aroma.

THE BLESSING FOR THIS GENERATION

R av Shimon Shkop *zt"l* said that Avraham Avinu had no father and no *rebbes*. He started to achieve all by himself. Rav Shkop said that in the time preceding Mashiach, there will be a period when people will come to Torah by themselves. They won't have a *rebbe*. They won't have a father who brings them to *cheder*. They will just come by themselves.

It says in *Tanach* "... and you, the mountains of Israel, you will produce your branches and carry your fruits ..." The *gemara* in tractate *Sanhedrin* says this means that when this happens, we will know that the Master of the World is going to end the exile.

The fruits of the mountains of Israel are not necessarily the oranges which grow in the orange groves. The fruits are the branching out of the yeshivos and the products of the yeshivos. They are branching out very fast. People are growing very quickly. The help from Above in this generation is greater than it was in the generations in Europe.

◈§ There is a *gemara* about Rabbi Akiva and his friend Rabbi Elazar ben Azaria, and Rabbi Yehoshua. They went to visit an old man, one of the old sages of their time, Rabbi Dosa ben Harkonos. He was very old and did not come to the *beis midrash* (study hall) anymore, and he did not know the new generation of scholars who were studying there.

This delegation came to visit him, and he knew only Rabbi Yehoshua, who was also an old man. Rabbi Akiva had started learning late, and Rabbi Elazar ben Azaria was a young man, so Rabbi Dosa didn't know them. When they came in, a servant announced that the sages of Israel had come to visit him. Rabbi Dosa invited Rabbi Yehoshua to sit. Rabbi Yehoshua then asked, "Rebbe, would you invite another one of your students too?" They had been learning his teachings, so he referred to them as Rabbi Dosa's students.

Rabbi Dosa asked, "Who is it?"

He said, "Rabbi Akiva."

Rabbi Dosa then asked, "Are you the Akiva whose fame is all over the world? May there be many like you in Israel."

There is another meaning to that *berachah* (blessing), besides the idea that there should be many scholars of Rabbi Akiva's caliber. It also means "may people *grow* like you in Israel."

Rabbi Akiva started learning when he was forty years old, and he became the great Rabbi Akiva. He must have grown very fast. He made up for forty years of not learning. So Rabbi Dosa ben Harkonos said, "Are you *that* Rabbi Akiva? I wish that many will grow as fast as you."

The late starters of today must have that blessing of Rabbi Dosa. They grow fast. There is a certain Divine assistance given to those who learn Torah in this generation, which is unlike that which was given to the last generation in Europe; there, growing in Torah took more time. Today there are many who are very advanced in learning, and they have made it in a short time. They must have that blessing of Rabbi Dosa.

BREAKING THE SHADES; SHINING THE LIGHT

The greatness of a person lies in the consistency of his understanding with his behavior.

I was in Brazil in 1953, and there was a *Yid* there who was a businessman, and not a big *talmid chacham* (scholar). But he radiated greatness, not unlike that which I had seen in some of the greatest people in my past in Europe. I had tremendous admiration for him. Someone asked me what I saw in him, and I explained with the example of an electric light bulb. If you take two bulbs and put them next to each other, but one has a lamp shade on it and one does not, then the one without the shade will give out the greater light. The shade covers up the light. The heavier the shade, the less light is given.

In our lives, we are used to heavy shades. We may have great understanding in our minds, but when it comes to our behavior and our character, the shade may be so heavy that very little of what we *really* are comes across. The light of our knowledge and understanding motivates a little, but the shade *distances* very much.

◦§ This man in Brazil was like a small bulb, but he had tremendous sincerity and he shone with a great light.

Today, this is all around. You find it very much with *baalei teshuvah*, those who have returned to Torah observance. Many others have a bigger bulb than they, but the *baalei teshuvah*, in order to return, have broken the shades, and that's why they often shine with much more light. Thank G-d, we meet them day after day.

Torah: Its Wonders and Gifts

The Rambam says that we should look around in the world for Hashem and observe His Creation. He says that the more we observe the Creation, the more we will fall in love with the Creator.

But then, in another place in his writings, the Rambam says that we should study His Torah, and the more we study, the more we will have love of Hashem. Thus he talks of two different ways of coming to love Hashem, and they go together. Unless I study and observe Torah, I won't have a good chance of marveling about an apple. Subjectively, an apple is good because I can eat it. Objectively, an apple is a marvel of Creation. Torah does something to me that shapes me in objectivity, and then I can truly observe the apple and be in awe of it, and of the rest of Creation.

There is a blessing we make: "... *borei pri ha'etz.*" ("Blessed are You, Lord our G-d, King of the Universe, Who creates the fruit of the tree.") In this blessing, we are saying, "I thank You," for the fruit. *But most of all, it means "I marvel."*

ON COMPREHENDING TORAH

In terms of *depth* of the Creation, there is no end. We can see this in a plain plastic box. If we simply look at it, it is merely a box we can make use of. But do we actually *know* the box? Do we consciously realize how many molecules and atoms are inside?

There is no end to the depth of anything that the Master of the World has created. This fact is true, also, with Torah. It is much deeper than what we learn on the surface. Its levels are infinite. It is, in fact, the greatest gift of the Almighty. If we don't realize this and we don't treat it as a gift, then we find only the shell. The "hidden" Torah, which is under the surface, is in the area of what are called "secrets of Torah," which are simply deeper and deeper levels of understanding, available to each person according to his level.

🙚 I was once walking with my father zt"l, when he told me something which he had heard from the Chafetz Chaim. The Chafetz Chaim said that all the Torah which the Vilna Gaon knew, together with all that of the Rambam, together with all the knowledge of Ravina and Rav Ashi, of Rabbeinu Hakadosh, of Hillel and Shammai, the Prophets, Yehoshua, and even all that Moshe Rabbeinu knew — all this together is so little compared to what there is in Torah that we say, "Toras Hashem temimah," the Torah of the Almighty is complete, as if it were untouched.

🙚 In order to enable us to understand the Torah, a creation without an end, the Almighty gave a very important gift along with His Torah: the gift of automatic adjustment. This is similar to how a mother nurses her child. An infant who is one day old doesn't have the strength to take as much milk as a child of two years, or the need for as much milk. Does the mother measure the milk for each of them? The Master of the World has created it so that the milk is automatically given according to the capacity of the child to receive. In the book Duties of the Heart, the author calls this one of the wonders of Hashem's Creation.

It is exactly the same with Torah. When a rebbe — a Torah teacher — gives Torah over to his students, if his only aim is that the students should know, then he has a blessing, just like the mother feeding her child. The rebbe's explanation adjusts itself to the student, and the student grasps it on his level.

The Mishnah in Pirkei Avos says that "it is not up to you to finish the work." One can imagine, for instance, a large park with a gate at the entrance. Once you go through the gate, you can go as far as your feet can take you. There is no end. You go as far as you can. This is what a gate of understanding is. It is an opening, and each person can go in. One gate leads to another, and it is endless. It's all different sections of Creation. The levels are infinite, and each grasps at his own level. What the Almighty wants from us is to *go*, to proceed as far as we can.

TORAH AND WATER

Sometimes when it rains, some fish jump, opening their mouths to catch yet another drop of water, even though they have plenty in the river. Yet they love water so much that when there is an opportunity to get a little more, they are eager for it and feel they can't afford not to get it.

The *Midrash* mentions this and compares the Jewish people to fish. Just as the fish, who *live* in the water, will attempt to get more, so will a Jewish person who is full of Torah run over to someone who says something that is true. The more a person is full with Torah, the more his ears are always open to hear — "Maybe somebody will say something good." A Torah person doesn't become satisfied. He is always looking for more Torah.

Our Rabbis often compare Torah to water. The *gemara* says that "there is no water except Torah." This refers to the fact that when the word "water" is mentioned in the Torah, it refers to Torah itself. It is written, for example, that Yaakov dug wells. This is referring to the fact that he established yeshivos. The Rambam also talks about this comparison and says, in the name of the Sages, that if you pour water on an incline, it goes to the lowest point. Similarly, words of Torah stick only to people who are humble and modest.

◦§ But there is more to it than that. The human body is made up mainly of water. It is a wonder of Creation that the Almighty took some water, gave it a nose, eyes, ears, a mouth; then He added some intelligence, and a human being resulted! If you take out the water, he would simply disappear, because he is almost completely made up of water.

This is what it really refers to when it is taught that "there is no water except Torah." Our entire essence and substance — the substance of a Jewish person and the Jewish nation — is Torah. Where there is Torah, there is life.

The key to everything Jewish is the learning of Torah. In the time of Rabbi Akiva, the Romans knew that. So did Hitler. He came into a location and searched out and destroyed the Rabbis, because he knew they were the future. In the time of the Romans, when they prohibited the study of Torah, Rabbi Akiva taught Torah in public. Pappus ben Yehuda, a great philosopher, admonished him and said he was endangering his life and the lives of others.

Rabbi Akiva told him the story of the fox who wanted to catch a fish for his dinner. Since he could not go into the water, he tried to coax the fish out of the river. He saw fish swimming and attempting to escape the fishermen's nets. The fox tried to persuade them to come ashore to safety. The fish said, "You are supposed to be a smart animal! Look at this situation: in our own element we are in danger; what will happen if we leave it?"

Rabbi Akiva was saying to Pappus, "You are a smart man, a great philosopher. We *live* in Torah. This is our life, and with this we are in peril. What will happen when we are outside of it?"

In fact, the *gemara* tells us that three days after the people crossed the Red Sea, the prophets among them — Moshe, Aharon, Miriam, and others — noticed that the unity of the people was starting to crack. They therefore instituted the public reading of the Torah on Shabbos, Mondays, and Thursdays. Thus, they made certain that the people would never be left for longer than three days without Torah. Originally, they established the minimum reading as three *pesukim* (verses) a day. Later, Ezra raised the minimum to ten. But Moshe Rabbeinu, together with his contemporary prophets, felt that public Torah reading at the ratio of one *pasuk* (verse) a day would suffice to preserve the unity of the Jewish nation. This demonstrates that one sentence of Torah is very powerful.

Every word of Torah that enters a Jewish person makes that person more *Yisrael*. It makes him greater. This is the joy of growth, and the Master of the World has given it to us out of His love for us.

❦   ❦   ❦

When a person comes into the yeshiva and is in the Torah element, he is literally in the water, and the water of Torah is full of tremendous force. Whether we realize it or not, when we swallow it we are taking that energy into ourselves, and it provides tremendous inspiration. But you won't reach its depth unless you learn it the way it was meant, unless you believe in it and you trust it.

TORAH AND INSPIRATION

For us, learning provides our inspiration. Wherever there is learning of Torah, there is inspiration, there is light, and there is continuation.

Once, when I was living in California, I wanted to create a summer program in the yeshiva there. I said to one of the students, "Reuven, I would like you to go to Tucson, Arizona, and canvass for some kids there." At that time, you had to go by train. He said, "I can't. I haven't learned for the last three days. I have no inspiration." He had been preparing some equipment for a camp. So I told him, "Go by overnight train. Take a *gemara* with you and study the whole night so the next morning you will be inspired." I didn't tell him, "You'll be rested," but "You'll be inspired." He missed the express train and took a local train, so he had even more time for his inspiration.

His reaction was the normal reaction of a person who studies Torah. If he doesn't learn for three days, he has no inspiration and can't inspire others. This is the realization of how much inspiration we find in each word when we learn Torah.

The Rambam says that if you meet people who have not been raised in the Torah way, don't expect them to become fully observant rapidly. He says that even if they are later exposed to Jewish communities and are still not eager to live according to Torah and all the *mitzvos*, don't blame them. That's the way they were raised. He goes on to say that it is a *mitzvah* to attract them with friendly words. With this, he refers to teaching them Torah through the stories of Torah and the things that do not require a commitment, until they come back to the strength of Torah.

There is a certain strength of Torah and a certain inspiration that simply needs to be tasted to be found. Then a person develops a very strong incentive to live up to Torah and to observe it. This requires *further learning*, in order to have the information necessary to live a Torah life. Even if a person is wise, he can do nothing without the information.

THE CANDLE AND THE TORCH:
THE FULLNESS OF JEWISH LEARNING

When we are learning Torah, there are two goals. One goal is learning itself, and the other is learning in order to be able to utilize the information for practical application of the *mitzvos*. The higher goal is the learning itself, for its own sake.

In the *gemara*, a *mitzvah* is compared to a candle, and the study of Torah is compared to light itself. The *gemara* understands that a person who is learning for the sake of knowing how to practice brings a light into the world. But it is still the light of a *candle*. It is not as big a light as that which is carried by one who studies just for the sake of study.

A candle focuses on one spot. When you have a candle burning, the room may be dark, but you can always direct the candle to that spot which you want to see. On the eve of Pesach, when we check our homes for *chametz* — leavened bread — we search only with a candle and not with a bigger light. This is because we have to focus on each and every spot, and a big light doesn't give an opportunity to notice every little detail. In fact, it distracts from the details.

On the other hand, when you use a candle, you don't see the scenery. You don't see the overall picture. You have information from the spot on which you are focusing, but you don't really understand it.

The candle is the *Shulchan Aruch*, the Code of Jewish Law. It focuses and it says, "Do it like this." In order to perform the *mitzvah*, I need the candle. It is the information which enables me to do the *mitzvah*. But it's not yet the fullness of Torah learning.

The *gemara* is the light which provides the larger picture. When I learn *gemara*, I not only have a candle in my hands, but I also become familiar with the entire scenery. Then my learning shines in a larger area and becomes a powerful light. I am using my brain just to *know*, just to have a picture in my mind of the Creation, so that the Creation lives also in *me*.

At the same time, I find out much information which I put to use. But in the fullness of Torah learning, I learn even subjects that have nothing to do with my practice.

When I learn *mesechta Kiddushin* (the tractate dealing with marriage), for example, most of it is theoretical. When a person gets married, he doesn't need the entire *mesechta*. He needs a good bride.

This idea is found in the business world. A person uses the income he earns to buy what he needs. But when he is working in his business, he is just producing income. Later, when he comes home and he has to make a *cholent*, he uses his income to buy the ingredients.

Torah information is not only information to make or do something specific. Torah information is for learning — it constitutes wealth. The main ambition is to become a wealthy person in Torah. But while I'm learning, I'm also storing away information for the time when I'll need it. Then when I need it, I take it out and I use it.

◦§ If someone would learn only *halachah* (practical law) all his life — using the candle, so to speak — he would still be walking in darkness. If a person wants to have the light of Torah in his mind, he learns *gemara*. In Chumash, after the *menorah* (candelabrum) had already been miraculously made, Moshe Rabbeinu was told, "... and look, and make ..." But where should he make it? It was already made. The answer is that he should make it in his mind. The function of the Torah is to bring light into the mind.

But if someone is learning Torah without the intention of practicing what he is learning — he is learning *only* with the big light — this is not even called Torah. It loses all its strength and life-force. There must be the intention to live up to what one learns. Even if he learns the laws of Pesach in the summertime, when he is not able to fulfill them, if he intends to fulfill them when their time comes around, *this* is valid Torah.

A person who learns *gemara* without intending to give it out, to *produce* with it — to perform *mitzvos* — has a Torah that is not alive. And the other person, who learns *only* to perform the *mitzvos*, has a living Torah, but not the fullness of Torah which he would acquire by learning *gemara*.

Thus, it is taught that "the *mitzvah* is a candle, and the Torah is light." Both the information in the *halachah* and the large scope which learning *gemara* provides are needed in order to reach the fullness of Jewish learning.

INTELLECTUAL MATURITY IN SEARCH OF THE WONDERS OF THE CREATOR

How do I know that each and every word in Torah is Divine? I know it because the wonders in Torah are so great, it couldn't be human. But in order to know this, you have to learn . . . and the more you learn, the more you see it.

How can we expect to understand the Torah, which is Divine and infinite, with human intelligence? Certain things are hidden because our minds are not prepared. These hidden things are too fine to handle with the tools which our minds presently have. So our intelligence has to be sharpened in order to be able to handle the concepts which deal with the finer aspects of the Creation. If we will try to force ourselves to understand ideas which are not on our level, we will definitely misunderstand, which is not Torah at all.

◦§ We say at the Pesach *seder*, "According to the knowledge of the child, the father instructs him . . ." It is very interesting that a major component of intellectual maturity is the power of imagination. This means that one doesn't have to see concrete things in order to understand them. He can imagine concepts. When you start to teach a child to count, he cannot understand the concepts of "one," "two," and "three." You must give him pencils. "One pencil, two pencils, three pencils . . ." The concept of "two," without having an *actuality* to it, needs a certain maturity. The more we develop, the more we can have concepts. That is the power of *imagination*.

◦§ The Rambam explains that when we learn Torah, we are developing and shaping our intelligence, which then enables us to receive even more Torah. The study of *gemara* is a grinding machine that grinds your brain, sharpens it, and prepares it for learning further. In his *Introduction to the Mishnayos*, he says that this is the purpose of learning *gemara*: to prepare our minds to understand more of *emunah* in Hashem, which is an opening to understanding the ways in which the Creator of the Universe operates in our world.

◈ Therefore, we have an immediate goal, and we have a remote goal. The immediate goal is learning for the sake of learning, and learning for the sake of fulfilling the *mitzvos*. The remote goal is to draw close to the Creator of the Universe, and this is also accomplished, explains the Rambam, through our learning.

We live in a period when there are so many people in the world who are observing and learning about the wonders of the Creation. Science is discovering and identifying many great things today, but the laboratory is not in competition with Torah. If science can tell us what we are *able* to do, Torah can tell us what we *should* do. Torah provides the bigger picture which tells us the *place* of the latest discovery in the total scheme of things.

In fact, instead of coming to awe of the Creator, many of those who learn about the newest discoveries go *away* from it. Therefore, to learn and to observe the wonders of the Creator, it is safer for us to learn a *Tosafos*, the great commentary on the *gemara*. It is *there* that we see the wonders of the Creator, in a depth without end.

One time I heard a young student discussing proofs of the fact that Torah was Divinely given — *Torah min haShamayim*. I told him, *Torah min haShamayim*? When I learn a sentence in the Chumash or a *Tosafos*, I see *Torah min haShamayim*, because it is absolutely impossible for that to be a human product. There is so much precision in it. There is so much of eternity in it.

WHAT IS GEMARA?

The system of learning Torah is a special and unique system. I haven't seen any system of learning which develops the brain as much as *gemara*. It is built on the principle that a person should work out for himself and discover for himself the information he needs. He is not given the information. He is given the material, and he is given the guidance to help him decipher it, but he has to find it himself.

This principle is also true in a science class. Instead of telling the law or the rule to the student, you let him perform an experiment and find out for himself. You could have saved the experiment and simply given him the information. But if you want him to have the maximum benefit of that information, you make him produce it himself.

That is exactly how Torah was given. It says in the Mishnah, "In the study of Torah you should toil." This is because Hashem wants us to produce the information, and then it will be part of us. It's all there, but we have to dig it out. That is what *gemara* is.

The first time that Moshe Rabbeinu taught the people in the desert, he did the same thing. He gave them a formula, and that formula was the Mishnah. With us also, when we open the *gemara*, we first have the Mishnah. The *gemara* then tries to discover what the Mishnah is telling us.

A good *gemara rebbe* tells his students as little as possible. He questions them and makes them reach conclusions instead of explaining everything. There is no straight road in the *gemara*. Somebody makes a statement; then you question it, you discuss it. In the *gemara* there are all kinds of questions and all kinds of answers. In the end, you come out with a very clear concept and with true intellectual maturity.

TORAH AND THE DEVELOPMENT OF THE PERSONALITY

> *As we learn Torah and draw closer, as the Rambam says, to understanding the ways in which the Creator operates in the world, we initially discover the wonderful taste of "chewing" Torah. But the real force and the real benefit of Torah is not in the "chewing" but in the "swallowing" of it. That means that if you learn Torah correctly, it is a living thing, and it penetrates the conscious and subconscious mind, whether you are aware of it or not.*

If we are not conscious when we are learning Torah that this is the same Torah that was given to us by the Creator of the Universe at Sinai, then we have taken all the life out of it.

But if we *do* learn Torah with the awareness of its true source, then we receive an injection of Torah straight into our systems. We bring so much life into ourselves that it straightens everything out. Similar to this is a plant which has roots; when the plant is growing in the soil, it has life. If someone comes and cuts off a branch, then from the minute the branch was cut off, it is dead. It may have value as a piece of wood, but it is not a living plant.

The root of all *Yiddishkeit* is Torah from Sinai. The whole personality of the Jewish person receives its sustenance from this root. When planted in that root, the Jewish person flourishes with Torah, with good character traits, with *mitzvos*, and with everything good.

People work in order to earn the money they need to live. The money is a means to an end. Often, after a person has more than enough money to live, he continues working. In fact, he often works with more force and ambition than he did when he started out. The money is no longer the *means*, it has become the *end* in itself. The person feels that he is receiving something essential, which is *more* than just the money.

We are taught in *Mishlei* (Proverbs) regarding the search for Torah wisdom, "If you seek it as you seek money . . ." When one seeks the knowledge of Torah, like a fish in water jumping for more even though it has plenty already, then the Torah becomes an *end* in itself, and the learner receives something that he considers essential, and his personality is developed as he learns.

A person in society is subject to many different influences, and he is not always able to separate his *own* thoughts and ideas from external influences. He cannot always think and examine issues independently. His ability to reason is often put under the control of his emotions. In fact, my father *zt"l* said that if not for our emotions, we would all be believers in Hashem. He said that belief is logical. Rabbi Akiva said that when you see a house, you are certain that someone built it, and when you see a garment, you are certain that a tailor made it. When you see a Creation that is so well organized, you also have to say that Someone made it and sustains it.

⊷ There is a story about a manufacturer who comes into the synagogue and offers the *gabbai* (sexton) a million dollars. The *gabbai* says, "What for?"

The man answers, "Not much. Just introduce in your synagogue the practice that whenever people have to say 'Amen,' they should say my product's brand name instead."

This is the way products and ideas are sold: by constant repetition. It is human nature to be susceptible to this. Many of the ideas that we have are not because we figured them out, but because we simply *accepted* them.

However, when you come into contact with people who study Talmud, you find people with intellectual maturity. In learning *gemara*, you analyze everything. You question everything. The more a person learns *gemara*, the more he develops the capacity for analysis. It shapes one's objectivity, and one develops the ability to be in control of his emotions rather than being controlled by them.

A person whose mind is not well developed is a very subjective person. The greater a person is, the more objective his mind is. From a subjective angle, an apple, for example, is good because I can eat it, and I am grateful to the Creator for giving it to me. This gratitude is a quality of extreme importance. Still, I am thinking of myself and what the apple means to *me*.

⋅⋅⋅ The person whose mind is well developed is able to see the apple for *what it is* in itself. It is — objectively — a marvel of Creation; and in the great man, his capacity to marvel is developed as well as his gratitude. Thus, this ability to *marvel* at the Creation also comes about through learning Torah.

Subjectivity leads to a preoccupation with one's *self*. We see in society that many people — whole cultures — are becoming corrupt and decadent as a result of the driven pursuit of self-satisfaction. The Ramban says that a person who is after self-satisfaction will get bored with his satisfactions and will constantly seek more ways to satisfy himself, until he destroys himself completely.

There must be aims other than self-satisfaction. When searching for people who have a very happy and meaningful life, one finds people who are led by Torah and build their lives with Torah. *Their secret is Torah*, and it works out.

The neighborhood where I live is an observant area. Everybody there learns Torah. There are professionals there, but everybody learns. It is full of children, and I watch hundreds of children playing there, and I have never seen a fight. There is love between the children, and it is the Torah life style that creates it.

◄§ I love the children in this neighborhood. I appreciate how they love each other. I see them walking together and holding hands. If a person is only for *himself*, then he does not give to the person he is with. They are two separate beings, taking from each other. But when a person is giving, at that moment he does not need to take, and the satisfaction and joy of giving is much greater than the joy of taking.

There are plenty of poor people there, but it does not affect the happiness. I was once asked to help distribute funds to families who were in great need. I was surprised to find that these particular families needed assistance. I knew them, and I had never seen any signs of unhappiness. It is in these homes that the Master of the World is building the Jewish nation. It is the learning of Torah that creates homes such as these.

For raising children, you need a lot of patience and a lot of love. Learning contributes to both. If a person is less subjective, he tends not to take things too personally and not to be tense and irritable.

Learning also creates satisfaction. The mind and the heart are constantly being inspired, and one is in a good mood and then can create love.

TORAH AND FREEDOM

The positive value of freedom of choice is not the freedom, but the ability to control it.

We say that the person who is occupied with Torah is a free person. Yet there seems to be a contradiction in this. If a person is in a place where there is no kosher restaurant and he is hungry, he stays hungry. Is he a free man?

There are many things that he is not free to do, yet we call him free. The answer is that he has enough controls to know what he can do and what he cannot do, and *real freedom lies in being in control*. In Chumash, Yaakov says to his oldest son Reuven, "You are hasty (unstable) like waters, and therefore you should not have authority." He was the firstborn, and he should have had authority over his brothers. Yaakov used the image of water to communicate to his son. A liquid cannot keep its own shape. It needs a container, and it takes on the shape of its container. A solid keeps its shape. So Yaakov says, "Because of your nature, which is like water, you cannot have it." In order to have authority, to be a leader, one needs highly developed self-control.

In a similar vein, the Rambam explains the verse in *Tehillim* (Psalms) "Do not be like a mule, who does not understand and has to be harnessed by bit and reins." An animal does not have the understanding to direct his movement in a way which will not cause damage. Therefore, if I have an animal, I can't let it walk around free. I have to harness and direct it.

"But you are human beings," explains the Rambam. "You have understanding, you have your minds. Figure out with your mind what you can do and what you cannot do. Control yourself, and there will be no need to put on controls from without."

◆§ This means that the positive value of freedom of choice is not the freedom, but the ability to control it. It is clear that it is essential that we learn how to control our freedom of choice, because today we have been given enough freedom to destroy the whole world in an instant. This is given to the human being.

◆§ The perfection of freedom of choice is what good character and behavior consist of. Good character must be learned. The Torah says that we have to change ourselves and train ourselves. The Torah gives us the ability and the tools to do this. Just as water must have a container, Torah learning has to have a container — a well-developed person. The character is the container for Torah.

The Rambam says that you train good character by repeating correct actions. One should keep on repeating such actions which are typical of a good character. After repeating an action several times, it will become part of you and part of your character.

An example of this is when someone needs help and I don't feel like doing it, but I know that I *should* feel like doing it. There is something wrong with my character. The solution is to help him anyway. Then the next time there is an occasion to help someone, I should help him too. If I keep on helping people, I will develop a feeling for other people. This is how you train your character, and while doing this, you go on with your learning.

When the Jewish people received their freedom, they were taken almost immediately to Mount Sinai, where they were given the Torah, which came with many intellectual and ethical tools for self-control and character development. Without this, the act of setting free 600,000 slaves could have been a very dangerous thing. Therefore, we see that this is the next step after, and the entire value of, freedom.

⋞ The Jewish idea of freedom does not consist of running wild. It consists of celebrating the making of a blessing; of recognition of the Creator of the Universe and our responsibility to place ourselves under His guidance and direction. Learning Torah brings that awareness into the conscious mind.

SHARING THE GIFT: THE CONTINUITY OF TORAH

No one knows what *life* is. Science doesn't know. Scientists can observe how life is produced, but *what life is*, and what is missing when a person passes away, they cannot identify.

It says in Chumash that the Master of the Universe created a corpse, and then he blew life into its nostrils. The life force is what the Almighty gave. The Torah is called *Toras Chaim* — a Torah of Life. It also has life in it, which came to us directly from the Almighty. It was given to Moshe Rabbeinu, who gave it to Yehoshua, and it was passed on further and further. Rambam lists all forty generations from Moshe Rabbeinu to Rav Ashi, who finally edited the *gemara*. Even though it was *edited* by him, it's all a long chain beginning with the Almighty and Moshe Rabbeinu.

When we learn Torah, we do not learn for ourselves alone. Each Jewish person is a link in that chain of receiving the Torah from the Almighty through Moshe Rabbeinu, and transmitting it to someone else, and so on to the next generation. That is why the *mitzvah* of Torah learning is not only to study it, but to study and to teach it. A person who learns Torah is a link in that eternal chain from the Almighty through the generations.

There is blood circulating throughout the body. If there is a clot in one place, it cannot go further. This is also true if Torah comes to a person and he stops it there. He doesn't let it go further. It's like a blood clot, because it's all one chain. The entire life of Torah exists because it comes directly from the Master of the World. Every word that we learn is from Hashem, and all the letters of the Torah are letters of Names of Hashem.

◦§ When Moshe Rabbeinu came down from the mountain and found the Golden Calf, he broke the Tablets he had received from the Almighty, and, in a sense, gave back the Torah. Even though he may have remembered what he had received, the Torah no longer had any strength, because the strength of the Torah comes directly from the Master of the Universe, and Moshe remained only with the *body* of Torah, without a life in it, and nothing to transmit.

Moshe Rabbeinu spent forty days, after he broke the Tablets, praying that the Almighty should forgive the Jewish People and give them back the Torah. He did not regret breaking the Tablets, but the people had done *teshuvah* (repented), and he wanted them to have the *life* which is in Torah.

THE GIFT OF GIVING

There is another beautiful gift that Torah gives, which is the gift of *giving*. The *Tanna d'vei Eliyahu* quotes a sentence from the *haftarah* of Yom Kippur which says that when you see someone who is hungry, you should break your bread and share it with him. The *Tanna d'vei Eliyahu* says that Torah is often compared to bread. Just as bread is the nourishment of the body, Torah is the nourishment of the soul. If somebody is hungry, he is undernourished. Even if you have just a piece of bread and not a full loaf, break a piece from that which you have and share with others. Learn something with him. Learn a sentence from Chumash. The one who takes from his Torah and shares with somebody who is less fortunate than he has the merit of help from Above that his own learning will become better.

Therefore, if someone asks how he can spare time from his busy schedule to learn with someone else, I say that if you help him with learning, then you have great compensation. *You* are actually the fortunate one.

◄§ All those who have found their way to Torah are the fortunate ones. In their merit, and in the merit of all those who sacrifice themselves, body and soul, for Torah, we pray that the Almighty will bring the time of redemption and salvation soon for each individual and for the entire *Klal Yisrael*.

Child-Raising and Education*

A child is like an immigrant who comes to a new country. He makes observations and adopts the customs of that country. If the parents are happy and they smile and help and cooperate with each other, the child learns that in that country, that's the way people are. So he also becomes like this.

SOME FUNDAMENTAL CONCEPTS

I have lived in the Mattersdorf section of Jerusalem for a number of years. There are many large families there, and the streets are full of children playing. I have never seen a fight. The parents are happy, so the children are happy, smiling, and friendly. You often see a number of children from one family going along together. Two are pushing a little carriage, and there's a little brother or sister inside, with some bags of food squeezed in also. The older ones may be carrying full shopping bags, and they are all watching out for each other and helping each other. It shows me that the parents don't fight, because if the parents did fight, the children would learn the skill!

---

*Editor's note: In reading this chapter, it should be remembered that Rabbi Wasserman and his Rebbetzin never had children. One of us once asked him how it was that he became such a particularly outstanding authority on the subject of child-raising; after all, an expert usually develops in a field in which he has personal experience. Rabbi Wasserman's unforgettable reply was: "I do have personal experience. I have the experience of how my parents raised me."

By the time a child is three years old, he already has a little brother or sister. By that age he's old enough to take some responsibility, so we train him to help the younger one. He becomes a *giver* at a very young age. When you have a child who wants to help, that is the greatest blessing. Raising children is a great occupation, and it has the greatest rewards. The first *mitzvah* (commandment) in the Torah is the *mitzvah* to reproduce. The Torah tells us that our fulfillment of that obligation does not end at all with bringing children into this world. It continues with bringing them up and making decent human beings out of them. The obligation to *raise* our children is not a separate *mitzvah*. It is an extension of the obligation to reproduce.

◆§ The successful fulfillment of that obligation brings *nachas* — happiness — and keeps parents and children together without a generation gap. In life we have our functions, and when we live up to them, it brings us happiness. One of the greatest of our functions is that of raising children, of raising generations. The most important thing to remember is that we have in our hands something which Hashem gave us to develop, to make into a worthy human being. The Torah does not want us to raise institutions. It wants us to raise *people*. The secret of raising people instead of institutions is unselfishness.

The efforts involved are compensated with a lot of joy, but the joy is not the goal. Many people think that everything in the world is to be enjoyed, even their children. So they bribe the child to do what they want, so that *they* will be happy. They want to get a smile from the child, so they bring him another toy. What they want is to *take* from the child, and thus the child also learns to take. He looks for what he can get from the parents. If he is not satisfied with what they give him, then he looks elsewhere to get what he wants, and he often rebels. But when the parent is a giver, the child is a giver.

A healthy relationship between people — whether friends or parents and children — consists primarily of one thing: How do I relate to the person next to me? Do I see him as someone that I want to *get* something from? Or is my concern with what I can do *for* him? When two people are together and each one is concerned with what he can do for the other person, it's wonderful. But if each one wants only to *take* from the other, it creates problems and it's the biggest tragedy.

To the parent who knows and understands his obligations to his child, everything he is doing as he is raising that child is for the benefit of the child, and not for his own self-interest. Many people have ambitions for their children which are selfish, and not for the good of the child.

There is a formula which is very simple: Raise the children for the children's sake. It's true that we are only human, and we cannot separate ourselves completely from our own self-interest. But the larger the degree of concern for the child, the more successful we are in raising him.

INTUITION IN CHILD-RAISING

Since parents need to be educators, why aren't they given courses in education before they marry?

The *gemara* answers this question when it says that "women have more *binah* than men." *Binah* is intuition; information which comes to us in such a way that we cannot trace exactly where that information came from, something like a calculator which gives an answer without telling you how it got the answer. We just have the information.

The Master of the World gave women a very strong sense of intuition because the mother has to be able to communicate with a newborn infant. The infant does not talk or understand words, but the mother feels his needs and finds ways to communicate with him. In the very early infancy period, the child is almost completely alone with the mother, and that's when there is the greatest need for intuitive communication.

In the same way, the Master of the World has provided all of us with a degree of intuition as an automatic guide. It is especially strong in the area of child-raising. We feel what is good for the children and what is not good for them.

But this flow of intuition is dependent on one very important thing: that our concern is for the child and not for ourselves. Once we are concerned for ourselves, then there is no communication. If you care just for yourself, the child copies you, and he cares only for himself. Then a generation gap develops. But as long as we are givers, then we have intuition to help in the shaping of the child to be a successful human being.

◄§ As we mentioned in our discussion on Torah teaching, Rabbeinu Bachya says that one of the wonders of Hashem's Creation is the relationship of the mother's flow of milk to the need of the baby. As the child grows, the flow adjusts itself and the child always gets just as much as it needs; not too little to starve it, and not too much to cause it to choke. In child-raising, this is the way our intuition enables us to give the child what he needs.

The *gemara* also refers to this essential concept. "More than the calf wants to be nursed, the cow wants to nurse it." We should not make a mistake and think that the cow has an urge to nurse the calf simply because she is heavy with milk. The cow does it because she has a feeling for the needs of the calf and a love for the calf that makes her want to feed it. It is not that the cow wants to give milk; it is that *she wants the calf to drink.*

In education, one's concern must be only for the child. If one's motivation is purely for the child, one will know how to teach. But if one has ulterior motives as well, then there is no guarantee.

> A young man approached me with the following question: His father was concerned that he should be able to make a living, and he was therefore considering going into Torah teaching. The question he asked me was: Should he take a course in education in order to learn how to be a teacher? When I asked him why he had chosen teaching, he said that he wanted to remain connected to Torah. I said to him, "If a person teaches with only the benefit of the students in mind, he will find that he has the personal resources to do the job. But if your motivation is primarily personal, if you are going into teaching for your own sake, I think you'd better take that course."

◄§ When we are parents, the Master of the World makes use of our sense of intuition, and in a natural way we are helped to communicate with the children, so that we know what they need and in what quantities.

METHODOLOGY: RIGHT AND LEFT HANDS

Chazal — our great Rabbis — state a most essential principle which is applicable to the relationship between teacher and student, and parent and child: "Always let the left hand push away and the right hand draw close."

Simply put, the principle for parents is that there must be a perfect balance between the left hand pushing away and the right hand drawing close. An extreme of one or the other can ruin the child and ruin the family.

The left hand represents the side of rigorous discipline, involving a number of elements. The right hand represents the side of tremendous affection and non-judgmental acceptance — unconditional love and acceptance. If both your hands are "left hands" and you use only discipline, then you end up simply pushing away. If both your hands are "right hands" and you express only love and affection, then you pull the child towards you, but you don't change him at all. But if the left hand pushes and the right hand pulls, you turn him around. By the properly balanced use of the two mechanisms, you are able to change the personality. These two aspects are what make a child perfect.

We are all children of Hashem, and that is how he deals with us. He gives us a tremendous outpouring of love but plenty of discipline. We have all experienced that.

Of course, even the discipline is a manifestation of love; a central tenet of our *emunah* as a nation is that when Hashem punishes us or sends us into *galus* — exile — or other difficulties, it is only because He loves us.

Likewise, in parenting, the most important thing to remember is that when balancing the love and the discipline, even the discipline has to be with love. We have to understand that whenever we establish discipline or rules or punishment, it is only out of the motivation of love. The discipline is just another way of manifesting kindness, because if you show too much kindness, you will produce just as big a ruin as if you give only discipline. Thus, the first thing the parent has to understand is that the discipline has to be totally for the sake of improving the child.

CONSIDERATION AND CONCERN

A parent must remember that there are two things that the child must develop in his personality; the parent cannot lose sight of them. The child must have *consideration* and *concern*.

Consideration means not doing anything which offends someone else. It is the ability to exercise self-control and limit oneself. A child needs to learn that from the very earliest age. The child has to know that he cannot do something which interferes. If the mother is resting, for instance, and cannot be disturbed, the child has to know what the rules are, and they must be strictly enforced.

Consideration means that before I do whatever I want to do, I have to know whether or not it meshes with whatever else is in the environment. A person has to learn that before he does anything, he has to test whether it is harmful or hurtful or interfering with anybody else.

Concern is what is called *chesed* — acts of kindness. It is not just a matter of limiting myself, but of going beyond that and going out and actively seeing what someone else needs. It's not enough that I am not interfering with somebody else, but now that I am not interfering and I am stable, let me take a look at the world and see how I can help.

It's not enough just to have a child who is full of self-control and doesn't interfere. You also need the child to have *chesed*, kindliness, and the motivation to go out and do what is needed.

This is also an extension of the principle of the interaction of the right and left hands. First, there is the self-control, the element of discipline, and then the going out and acting with kindness.

TEACHING SELF-CONTROL

The main thing the parents have to give the children is *character*. When it comes to applying discipline, there are two possible motivations which the parent could have. If the child is making noise, for instance, you may feel that this is a time for discipline. So you shout. But you may do it so that the child learns how to be quiet and considerate, or you may do it because *you* want quiet.

The two possible ways in which you can go about doing this, including your tone of voice and your physical gestures, may be worlds apart. The effects on the child of the two motivations may also be worlds apart. If you shout because *you* deserve peace and quiet, delivering the message that "this child can't even keep quiet for half an hour," you teach him, through your outburst of anger, that *you* are expressing your needs in anger. He learns selfishness from that. He doesn't learn to be quiet as he should.

It's not easy when it's a few hours before Shabbos and the mother is running around preparing and a little child is pulling on her skirt and she wants to get rid of him at that moment. She should realize that she should not be so concerned about making that *cholent*. She should be concerned that the child learn not to disturb her. The child won't learn it if she just yells at him and says, "Go away!" First, you have to take a deep breath and maintain the self-control that's needed to discipline that child — to teach him how to keep quiet because *he* needs to learn how to be quiet, not because you need silence. Your tone of voice and your mannerisms will be different. What the child sees is also a completely different thing. He sees a parent who is in control, and who is teaching the child something that the *child* needs to learn.

> Somebody came to the Steipler Gaon and asked him what to do about his boy. He said, "I don't know what to do anymore. I keep on beating him and I can't correct him."
>
> The Steipler answered him, "What I *can* guarantee you is that he will grow up to be a beater."

◆§ One should never get angry, but if you are angry, that is not the time to act. Often when a person is angry, he cannot exercise the right judgment, and he fools himself into thinking that he is right.

◆§ It is a basic principle that you save so much energy and worry if you are consistent in everything. Generally, once you have a rule, don't give in. There are times, though, when we do have to give in. We are humans, and we have situations which demand that we exercise kindness at that moment. But if your line is not sharp, then you have no line at all.

In my parents' home there was tremendous warmth and affection. Yet our mother, *aleha hashalom*, had a rule that we could not ask for anything. If we asked for something, we didn't get it. We didn't have much money in our house, and our parents wanted us to know that they didn't have. The message was, "If we can afford, and we have, you'll be given. We know what you need," and we felt confident in this. This taught us self-control and gave us a sense that we would be given what we needed. We learned that we couldn't walk around being *wanters* and *takers*.

One day, our mother came home with some honey. My younger brother Dovid, *alav hashalom*, was four years old at the time, and he wanted some. But he knew that if he would ask for the honey, he'd never get it. So he moved a chair over to the table, got up on the chair, and made a *berachah* "*shehakol*" (the blessing made on various foods, including honey) in a loud voice. This way, my mother would be obligated to bring him some honey because he had pronounced a blessing and one must not make a blessing in vain. Her response was that she went to the kitchen and brought him a glass of water!

It is very important that children learn that there are things they can do and things they cannot do. I remember that I wrote a letter to my niece who had a daughter about two years old. I addressed the daughter and said, "Tell Ma she should not give you whatever you want. She'll spoil you."

Consistency is the best way of teaching self-control. Once you've said something, try not to change. You have to be careful in the first place of what you say, but once you say it, you should stay with it.

ON THE FAMILY

Learning Torah is very important for the raising of children. A father who learns has an easier time with child-raising. For us, learning is our life and the flavor of our life. The children see that the father is learning, and that's an inspiration.

It's very important that the husband and wife help each other in preserving the home. They need to work together.

It doesn't hurt to have little meetings in the family from time to time, to discuss some of the problems objectively. "Here is a problem. What can we do about it?" In almost every problem, there is some little opening which allows you to do something. Then you can all try together to work and solve the problems.

We should try to talk to children as adults, not in baby talk. Often, we underestimate the capacity of children. We *can* make them think like adults. They *can* learn consideration for others, which is a definite sign of maturity.

If the child did something that was not right, you can call him in a day or two later and say, "Remember how this and this happened," in a very friendly way, like talking to an adult and explaining something that is not right. "This is something that is better for you to stay away from." This is a nice way of training someone.

It is preferable to say things to a child in a positive way rather than to insult him; one is much more likely to be heard when one appeals to the positive side of a person. For example, one should not say, "You are a bad boy." It is much better to say, "For a good boy like you, that act was not appropriate." A little "*schmaltz*" helps!

⋖ It's very important always to have a smile for the child. Always be friendly. Take him in your hands. Even when you say "No," it should be friendly. The Rambam says that sometimes you have to *act* as if you are angry. But that's when you are not actually angry.

The child needs to feel that he has acceptance and somebody to lean on. This helps the child to accept the all-important *mitzvah* of *kibud av v'em* — respecting the parents. This *mitzvah* should be impressed on the child as much as possible, because without *kibud av*, the Divine Presence does not rest in the home.

⋖ Teachers also need to develop the same attitudes toward their students. If the students develop a pleasant relationship with their teachers, it is obviously much easier for them to accept their teachings. The *rebbeim* (teachers) in the yeshivos often have this kind of relationship with their *talmidim* (students). Secular teachers seldom do.

A man who had been head of the history department in a large American university for fifty years came into a yeshiva one day to say *kaddish* (the memorial prayer). He was talking to the Rosh Yeshiva and he said, "Rabbi, I am a lonely man at this point in my life."

The Rosh Yeshiva was surprised. He asked him, "How many students did you teach in your life?"

They made a general accounting and came up with a figure of 30,000. So the Rosh Yeshiva asked him, "Out of 30,000 students, did any of them ever invite you to their wedding?"

The professor said, "No. Not one."

That's very interesting. Probably not one student in a *yeshiva* would ever think of having a wedding without inviting his *rebbe*. This is because Torah is given *b'ahavah* — with love — and it creates a close relationship between student and teacher. A general principle in teaching Torah subjects is that the students should be thought of as the teacher's children. Only Torah creates this kind of relationship, and it does so in a natural way.

It says in *Tanach* (Scripture) that at the end of time, Eliyahu will come, and his job will be to bring back parents to children and children to parents. This indicates that there will be a time when the gap between parents and children will be one of the most serious tragedies. It could be talking about our time.

∽§ The more correctly we live, the happier we are. Everyone would agree that those delinquents who are coming up like mushrooms today are the unhappiest kids in the world because they are definitely on an incorrect path.

The most important thing to remember is that from the minute we have the child, we have to know that our job is to help him and make a *mentsch* out of him, and Hashem will help and we will find our way.

Living in the World

TRADES AND SKILLS

The *Ribono Shel Olam* (Master of the World) has created human beings in such a way that each person cannot provide for all his needs by himself. One person cannot be a tailor, and a carpenter, and a builder ...

Therefore, human beings have been created as social beings, and people have to help each other and exchange skills and products. Each person is a consumer and a producer. The consumption encompasses a wide area and the production is limited. A tailor's production is clothing, but his consumption is *everything*. He uses his one skill as an exchange with everybody else for their productions.

It is an obligation for a person to prepare himself for a line of production. If we consume and we do not produce, we are parasites. According to Torah law, a professional gambler is disqualified as a witness because he is a taker and not a giver. He is a consumer and not a producer. *Production* is a very basic condition of every human being.

It is interesting that there is an opinion in the *gemara* that merchandising (acting as an agent) is not considered production. The merchandiser seems to act between others who perform actual acts of production. The middleman has been called a parasite. But we rule that it *is* production. The reason for this concerns the fact that one of the major underlying concepts of the laws of Shabbos is the idea of *production*. When one writes, he produces something. When he erases, he produces writing paper. All the *melachos* (prohibited creative actions) of Shabbos involve production. Carrying outside of one's domain on Shabbos — one of the *melachos* — involves transportation of goods, which is an extension of production. If a *siddur* (prayerbook) is printed and wouldn't have a bookseller to sell it, it would remain in the print shop.

If one has a piece of paper in one place and he can't use it there, he has to carry it to the place where he wants to use it. Therefore, the carrying brings it closer to its usage, although he doesn't change the nature of the paper itself. It was a paper before and it is a paper now. Nevertheless, since merchandising brings it closer to its intended use, it is considered production.

People who spend their whole lives learning Torah also do not seem to be producing any material benefit for others. But learning Torah is in the category of those acts which are a completely Jewish kind of contribution: a total *giving*.

A Torah scholar causes all of the Jewish people to become rich. In economics, there is the sphere of the individual's domain and the sphere of the community's domain. When it comes to the total national wealth, it does not make a difference to the wealth of the nation, in one particular sense, whether that wealth is concentrated in a few hands or distributed equally among everyone. The nation is still wealthy. And a wealthier nation can accomplish more. Even a poor man who is living in a wealthy nation has certain advantages.

It is exactly the same in the Jewish community. When someone is learning, he is adding to the public good with his learning. The Torah scholar adds to the accumulation of Torah and causes the whole nation to become rich. When the Chafetz Chaim lived, all the Jewish people were rich. When he passed away, the entire nation became poorer.

We have a responsibility to the Jewish people to become great in Torah. In the days of the Talmud they had *yarchei kallah* — people who were away from the yeshiva for ten months of the year came to the yeshivos for the month of Nissan in the spring and Tishrei in the fall. All the tradesmen and businessmen came to the yeshivos to learn. There is an obligation for a Jewish person to set a daily time for learning, but the *yarchei kallah* was much more than that.

TORAH AND PARNASSAH (EARNING A LIVING)

The Rambam says that the norm was for a person to work three hours a day. Perhaps in his day it required less time to provide for one's daily sustenance. The principle was that Torah should be combined with work in order to earn enough money to be able to learn that day. According to this principle, any other occupation which is not for producing a living for this day is considered an interruption of learning; the learning is seen as being of the utmost importance and providing for the riches and well-being of the whole nation.

When Hillel was working, was he still "Hillel the *tzaddik*"? He wanted to learn, but he could not learn unless he chopped wood, because he needed half of his wood in order to make a living, and half to sell in order to earn the small fee required to enter the *beis midrash* (yeshiva study hall). So his chopping wood was part of the day's learning, it was not an interruption, and he remained Hillel the *tzaddik*. Likewise, in the *halachos* of *netilas yadayim* (washing the hands before the meal), interrupting for the needs of the meal is not considered an interruption. But if my chopping wood is for next year, it's a problem.

The Rambam himself was not able to hold to the norm of working three hours a day. Originally, he and his brother settled in Egypt. His brother was a wealthy businessman and supported him. Then a tragedy occurred — his brother drowned and most of his fortune went with him. So the Rambam had to support his family, and he became the ruler's personal physician. He wrote a letter in which he describes his day: He spent the whole day in the palace, taking care of the royal court. When he came home in the evening, he was exhausted and hungry. But the house was full of people. Some were sick; some came for help, some for recommendations, and so on. He would apologize to them that he was tired and would see them as he lay in bed. On Shabbos afternoon, he would have meetings with the leaders of the community about community problems. Then he would teach the people. Then after Shabbos it would start again. So it seems that the Rambam held that working three hours a day and learning the rest of the time should be the ideal way, but if someone has a greater responsibility, then he cannot ignore it.

The idea is that although supreme importance is placed on the learning of Torah, *parnassah* is important. The *gemara* talks of its special importance: "Be careful to have produce in your house, for if there are disagreements, it is because of shortage . . . Rav Papa says . . .'When the barley is out of the container, disagreement knocks at the door and enters.' "

◆§ My father *zt"l* said that a person has to have a trade, but that you should know that just as when you learn Torah, you learn *lishmah* — simply to know — if you go to college to learn a skill, you should go *not lishmah*. You have to remember that you learn there not because you want to know. You learn because you want to learn a skill, to use it as a tool.

It means that you learn chemistry in order to be able to make a living from chemistry. While you study chemistry, you have no business to be a poor student. You have to be the best possible student. But your objective is that it's leading to a practical end. Learning for the sake of learning is reserved for Torah studies.

But my father attached the condition to it that you should not learn *apikorsus* (anti-Jewish ideas) such as evolution. In many colleges today this is almost impossible. You are required to take courses such as these, and he was not in favor of going to college under those conditions.

TORAH KNOWLEDGE AND SECULAR KNOWLEDGE

There is a very interesting *gemara*. It says that Avraham Avinu *davened Minchah* (prayed the afternoon service) at *exactly* noon. Today, we cannot *daven* before a half-hour after noon. The *gemara* says that this is because Avraham was a great astronomer and could recognize when it was exactly midday, but in the days of the *gemara* they didn't have clocks or watches, so they had to calculate, and an average person could have made a mistake. Therefore, they had to wait a half-hour to be sure. But Avraham knew exactly. The *gemara* also says he was a great *talmid chacham* (Torah sage) and was learning all the time. The *gemara* is saying that if you are a great *talmid chacham*, you don't need to study astronomy separately in order to know what is needed.

The Chafetz Chaim was also on the level of understanding many things without having to study them. We would go to hear him every Shabbos, during the *seudah shlishis* (the third Shabbos meal). He lived in a little house in Radin, and the entire yeshiva would come to listen to him. Thirty or forty people would squeeze themselves into the house, and the rest would stand outside and listen through the window. Every Shabbos, Reb Moshe Landinsky, the retired Rosh Yeshiva there, would come in and say, "*Nu!* When is Mashiach coming?" The Chafetz Chaim would start talking. He would say something from the Torah portion of the week, and it was connected exactly with what was going on that week in the world. I used to wonder how the Torah knew what would be happening. Now I think I understand.

"My words," says Hashem, "are like a flame, and like a hammer which pounds away at a rock and sends out sparks." A flame is one, but the sparks go in different directions. That is how Torah is. It has the total image, as when you look at the whole flame, and when you break it down, each and every part of it has its own message, its own spark.

When you learn Torah, first you need to get the entire picture, the *p'shat*. You see that the sequence of all the sentences makes sense together. But if you place it under a magnifying glass, each and every letter has a story. Each and every letter has a message.

There is a form of Jewish artwork in which a scene is painted which is composed entirely of text. There is, for example, a *Magen David* which consists of the text of the Scroll of Esther. There are two approaches to the picture. If you look from afar, you see the *Magen David*. If you come close and you take a magnifying glass, then each part has a message. You can see a sentence or word in the Scroll. Those great in Torah have a more powerful magnifying glass and find more sparks.

◄§ There is another aspect involved in discovering the deeper knowledge of Torah. This involves more than just the wisdom of the Torah. My father said that the limitations of our perceptions and our grasp are limitations of the body, not of the soul. The heavier the body is — the more it is concerned with *itself* — the more limitations it has. It creates *mechitzos* (barriers) that are limiting.

There were many occasions on which those who were close to the Chafetz Chaim saw clearly that he knew things that were impossible for a normal person to know. He could look at a person's face and know that person's past, present, and future.

The Chafetz Chaim did not feel for himself at all, so there was no *mechitzah*. He perceived things that other people could not see or feel. The Rambam also talks about this. He says that the body is the *mechitzah*, and the more material the life a person lives, the more *mechitzos* he has. If somebody makes his body holy, and everything he does is *l'shem Shamayim* — for the sake of Heaven — then he has fewer *mechitzos*.

The Chafetz Chaim was awesomely great in this. There are many stories about him that illustrate his great vision. For example, he passed away in the fall of 1933, just at the beginning of Hitler's rise to power, but he foretold what would happen. Once, before Hitler came to power, he suddenly burst out crying. He said, "I see that a war is coming and that the First World War will be like child's play compared to the one that is coming, and that people will suffer without an end." On other occasions he also alluded to this.

JEWISH AND NON-JEWISH CONTRIBUTIONS TO SOCIETY

The non-Jewish *(Bnei Noach)* contribution consists of a give-and-take relationship. It is part of the normal way of life that a person works and produces, and exchanges his products or skills with someone else. In truth, he is not adding anything, but he is not taking anything either. He exchanges production for production. He takes from society and he gives back to society.

The Jewish people, however, have a different type of relationship to production. Our duty is to contribute without taking. We have the *Bnei Noach* contribution also, in order to be able to exist. But this is not enough. A Jewish person is not working in order to be able to eat and eating in order to be able to work. It is not a vicious circle. We live for something. We eat in order that we may exist and in order that we may carry out our responsibilities to our Creator. Those responsibilities involve setting fixed times of learning every day, giving charity, performing acts of kindness, exerting oneself to raise children in the way of Torah. These acts are various kinds of contribution. They all involve a contribution without taking.

THE FUNCTION OF AMBITION AND APPETITE

"You open Your hand and You give to every living being . . ." The Master of the World has organized everything so that we have all that we need. But that is not enough; if we have food but we have no appetite, we will starve. So the Master of the World gave us also the will to eat.

The Rambam says, "Were it not for people who behave as if they were insane, there would be no world." A person who wants to become wealthy generally has to expand his business greatly. In the time of the Rambam, local trade could not generally make a person rich. Thus it was necessary to spend a lot of time traveling on the high seas. At that time, the transportation facilities were not like today. Ships were not as pleasant as they are today. The Rambam gives a picture of a man who wanted to make a lot of money — he had to spend most of his years at sea. He didn't enjoy his food. He didn't enjoy his family. He didn't enjoy his whole life, and he was always exposed to all kinds of dangers.

Eventually he became an old man and retired. He came home and had a lot of money. What did he do with that money? He started building a suitable dwelling for himself. In those days it took much longer than today to build a building. He was not sure if he would even live long enough to inhabit the building which he had begun. Thus, society benefits from his labor, but he does not. This is what the Rambam means when he says that such a person is acting like an insane man, and the world needs him.

This appetite and ambition is what Hashem has instilled in us. A shoemaker makes shoes not because he does not want people to walk barefoot. He makes shoes because he has an appetite to eat. But Hashem uses him in order to provide shoes for people. He has given us ambition, but the wise ones realize that, in truth, we are not working for ourselves, but for others.

❧ Shlomo Hamelech (King Solomon) describes the *Bnei Noach* contribution in the Book of *Koheles* (Ecclesiastes), when he says, "The sun rises, the sun sets ... all things go to the ocean, and the ocean is not filled." Then he talks about the wind which goes around in circles, and he says that the Creator of the World has created things to move in circles. The sun moves in a circle. (We know that it is the earth which moves, but in the way that we perceive it, it is the sun which moves.) Water moves in a cycle. The ocean doesn't fill up because it is also involved in circular motion; when we use the water, we return it to the ground, and the ground filters it and the cycle continues.

❧ Why does the sun move? Why does it move at precisely the rate that it does? We know that if it would slow down or speed up, it would be impossible to live on this earth. It would become terribly hot or unbearably cold.

Thus, the sun moves not because the sun needs it, but because the earth needs it. *Koheles* is describing the *Bnei Noach* contribution and the Rambam's discussion of the maintenance of the world: The world is made in such a way that everything is maintained through circular motion, and this is good. But the Jewish contribution is more than that. It is referred to as "a portion for yourself, and a portion for Hashem." A Jewish person organizes himself and devotes a part of his time for the *Bnei Noach* type of production and a part of his time for Torah and *mitzvos*. There are guidelines given by the Rambam and others which assist one in organizing his time along these lines.

TEACHING AND THE RABBINATE AS A TRADE?

There are times when a person reaches a certain level in Torah such that the community needs his leadership, and he is not free from it. He cannot become a watchmaker, for example. What benefit will the community have from all his watches? He must be a teacher of Torah. He does it not because he is interested in making a livelihood. He does it because he is obligated to lead. This is how a person should

*enter the rabbinate. Afterwards, he is compensated for
his time, so that he will be able to live.*

In Russia, under the influence of the *maskilim* (the
so-called "enlightened ones"), there was a group of Jews
who wanted to assimilate with the Russians. They went
to the Russian government and said, in reference to the
Torah scholars, that "they are Jews and they are not part of
the broader society, and you have to make them a part.
Their rabbis are standing in the way, so *you* train the
rabbis."

So the Russian government opened two "rabbinical
seminaries," one in Zhitomer and one in Vilna.

At that time, the well-known Rabbi Yisrael Salanter was
in Vilna, and they wanted him to become the head of the
seminary. He refused, and the government ran him out of
town. In the end, those seminaries produced the kind of
rabbi which the government recognized as rabbis, but the
community didn't see anything in them. The government
gave every community one of those rabbis, and he kept the
records of births, deaths, and so on.

Once, a religious man asked Rabbi Yisrael Salanter why
he had not accepted the job in the rabbinical seminary.
The behavior of the boys in the seminary had given them
a very bad reputation. When Reb Yisrael pointed that
out, the man said to him, "You, and other people of high
caliber, did not accept the position, and that's what happened."

Reb Yisrael explained why he had not taken the position:

"In the yeshiva, we never prepared for anything. A *Yid*
has to learn Torah, so we learned Torah. We studied simply
because we loved Torah. Then, when we grew and
developed the abilities to serve the community, we did it
because that was our duty. We are compensated for our time
so that we can carry out our obligation, but our objective is
serving the people.

"From the minute that you take people to prepare them
for the rabbinate as a trade, as a means of earning a living
for themselves, you corrupt the rabbinate, and no good can

come of it." Even if they would have made Reb Yisrael the Rosh Yeshiva, it would not have helped.

◦§ The shoemaker plies his trade in order to get in exchange what he needs to exist. Although he benefits others, his immediate motivation is the satisfaction of his own needs; but teaching should not be like this. A teacher's only motivation should be the good of the student. The student *must* have what he needs. If the teacher has more than one motivation, he does not go in a straight line.

Therefore, Moshe Rabbeinu said, "I taught you Torah the way that Hashem taught me. I did not have to pay tuition; the Holy One, Blessed is He — my Rebbe — did not charge me tuition. When you go to teach Torah, do not charge."

Do not confuse goals. If you do something for yourself, do it for yourself. If you do it for someone else, do it for *him*. But don't do it for yourself and convince yourself that you do it for him.

◦§ But how should teachers support themselves?

The *Shulchan Aruch* (Code of Jewish Law) has a formula. The teacher does not charge you for what he is doing; he is being compensated for the fact that during the time he is giving you, he is not doing anything else.

Dr. Breuer *zt"l* was the head of the German Jewish community in New York. Prior to that he was the head of the community in Frankfurt. He went to school and received a diploma as a college teacher, but he never used it. He went straight to the rabbinate. He was very honest, and he said, "If I want to be compensated for my time, my time should be worth something."

If a person feels that he can contribute by learning with people, by teaching, by heading a community, he should be ready to sacrifice and say that he is going to do something which will not pay him in exchange for his services, but which will compensate him for the time which he sacrifices.

My younger brother was a very great Torah scholar. When the time came for him to start looking for a marriage partner, I was living away from home. He wrote me a letter in which he said he was certain he had to marry a very poor girl. He felt that he had to be a Rosh Yeshiva. He said that if he would be anything else, he would feel like a soldier running away from battle. As a Rosh Yeshiva, he would not be able to live a comfortable life. My father was a Rosh Yeshiva, and our home was very poor, as were most of the homes of the Roshei Yeshiva. He felt he had to marry a girl who was not used to comforts. Eventually, that was the kind of person he married. That is the kind of dedication that is required of one who wants to serve. He must be completely dedicated to serving the *people* and not *himself*.

⋞ The great Torah scholars are like parents. They are concerned with, and want to have *nachas* from, each and every Jewish person. In the *gemara*, there is the case of a person who makes a business deal and then backs out of it in such a way that it causes harm to someone else, but it is all done in such a way that he cannot be held halachically liable for it, although it is unethical. It says that the scholars "do not have *nachas* from him." The leaders of Israel want to have *nachas* from every Jew.

In my generation, we had the merit to know a man who was the father of every Jewish person: the Chafetz Chaim. When he wrote the book entitled *Chafetz Chaim*, it concerned him that there might be a Jew somewhere who was not careful with his speech and was speaking *lashon hara* (forbidden speech). In his book *Nidchei Yisrael*, he wrote especially for immigrants to America and South Africa. The Jews had tremendous trials when they arrived in these countries. He very clearly expresses the trials that people faced there, especially at that time before the First World War. In that book, he had a section on *halachos*, and the *halachos* are the absolute minimum, with no stringency at all, in order to make it as easy as possible for the people to hold onto their Jewishness. He wrote a book, *Machaneh Yisrael*, for the soldiers in the Czar's army. Every Jew was his concern. He was communicating with every Jewish person through his books.

Shlomo Hamelech is a *rebbe* of the Jewish people. He addresses everyone as "my child." He says in the Book of Proverbs, "Guard carefully the command of your father and do not neglect the teaching of your mother." The Vilna Gaon says that "the command of your father" refers to the *mitzvos*, and "the teaching of your mother" to the Torah. Not only the great teachers, but the Torah and *mitzvos* themselves are considered our parents. Just as the

Torah and *mitzvos* are pure and come only to educate and elevate us, so do the greatest leaders and best parents have only one motive in mind: to help the student or child to mature into the very best person possible. This is the basis of all teaching. The welfare of the other is the *only* concern. The teacher must *not* see his profession as a trade, in the same way that a shoemaker sees his. He doesn't teach *because* he wants to have *nachas* from his students or children. But the *nachas* comes automatically.

Prophecy and Revelation

A vision is something which is seen, but not with the physical eye. Prophecy was not experienced through one of the five senses. It was a sixth sense.

"The prophecy of Moshe is not founded upon signs ... but with our eyes we saw and with our ears we heard the Divine Voice, even as he also heard it ... like persons who witnessed an event together." This is what the Rambam says.

THE PREPARATION FOR DIVINE COMMUNICATION

During the period of the infancy of the Jewish people, they went through several distinct periods.

The first one was when they became a nation. This occurred in exile in Egypt, where they underwent terrible tortures. It could be said that there they were in a very unhappy and tragic ghetto. But that is where they became a nation. They came into that ghetto as a *family*, and they came out a *people*.

The next period was a time of training in beliefs. It lasted for one year, the year prior to their leaving Egypt. The entire year was dedicated by Providence to implanting in their minds three basic beliefs: 1) the existence of Hashem; 2) that Hashem is concerned with human behavior; 3) that there is such a thing as Divine communication with a living human being, which is *prophecy*.

These three things were demonstrated time and again during that year before they came out of Egypt. For the entire period during which Moshe was negotiating with Pharaoh, everything was done in a miraculous way. Everyone knew these were things that could not be done by a human being. Eventually, as it says in Chumash, even the wise men of Pharaoh said, "This is the finger of G-d." The events showed the existence of G-d, and they showed His concern about what is going on here. The fact that Moshe predicted precisely what was going to happen, to the split second, demonstrated that there is some kind of communication with a human being.

The Rambam discusses this last aspect. He says that among the nations there are certain people who have an ability to predict things. But whatever their predictions are, they are never precise and are thus not a demonstration of prophecy. If they are precise, then they cannot come from a natural, human source. The predictions of Moshe Rabbeinu were in a completely different category from those of the "predictions" of the nations. His were extremely precise.

This is of the utmost importance, because these three basic beliefs, culminating with the demonstration of prophecy, were the necessary preparation for the giving of the Torah. If one does not accept that there is a possibility of Divine communication with a human being, then he would consider that whatever Moshe gave us is man made. Then the Torah loses all its value.

⊷ The entire value of the Torah is that it is not a human product. It is very hard for people who have never experienced it to understand that, but the more one becomes familiar with Torah, the more one realizes that it could not possibly be a human product. But it takes experience with it, and knowledge of it, to understand this fact.

Analogous to this is a piece of artwork. There are some people who are expert and can identify the artist. But you have to know something about it. If not, anyone can come and bring you any copy and tell you that it is an original.

We are so ignorant — we handle so many things, and we do not recognize the artist. There is an entire universe and we are familiar with many parts of it, although the fact remains that what we do not know is much more than what we do know. But we know a great deal. Yet we still don't recognize the artist.

A person simply has to examine what is going on in the tip of his finger, where he has blood vessels, nerves, little muscles, and see how perfect everything is and how it is all constantly reproducing without end. A physician can tell how precise the machinery is. Yet people still do not recognize that there is an artist behind it.

With that kind of attitude, a person could look at the whole created universe and still not recognize its greatness. But if anyone would tell me that such a thing could be a human product, I wouldn't believe him. And if anybody would tell me that such exquisite precision is just an accident, I definitely wouldn't believe him.

However, this is what they are taught in the public schools, and it is not logical.

When we learn Torah, the same idea is true. For us, it is clear that it is not a human product. There is so much precision in it. There is so much of eternity in it. It doesn't age. It's impossible for it to be a human product.

Before the Jewish people received the Torah, they had to be prepared for accepting it. They had to be given the basic knowledge, which was done during the period of training in beliefs.

FROM SLAVES TO PROPHETS "ON EAGLES' WINGS"

Just seven weeks before receiving the Torah, which was a prophetic experience shared by the whole nation, they were slaves. The distance between a slave and a prophet is very great. A prophet has to be a very great person. Even after the year's training in beliefs prior to leaving Egypt, they were still slaves, and far from the prophetic experience.

It is written that Hashem says, "I carried you on eagles' wings and I brought you to Myself." There are two aspects to this. One is the aspect of *protection*. The eagle flies the highest of all birds and carries its young above it, thus providing the best protection for its little ones. Other birds can be attacked from below by arrows or from above by other birds. But the eagle flies so high that there is no other bird flying over it.

So the Almighty is saying, "You can see that I gave you superior protection," because they went through all kinds of dangers.

The other meaning of "eagles' wings" is that the eagle is a fast flying bird. It symbolizes speed. It was essential that the Jews experience lightning-fast schooling to prepare them for being great enough to receive the Torah. Otherwise, as free people without Torah, chaos would have resulted, as is happening in so many places today.

After the people had all the fundamental beliefs demonstrated when leaving Egypt, the Almighty told them, "I am not a stranger to you. You have *experienced* things which are faith to other generations. But to you it was experience. I carried you on eagles' wings."

PROPHECY BY "PROOFS"; PROPHECY BY EXPERIENCE

At the giving of the Torah, the Jews were all prophets. Just prior to this, the Almighty says, "I am coming in a thick cloud, in order that the people of Israel should hear what I am saying to you, and they will trust you forever."

The Rambam, in his *Hilchos Yesodei HaTorah* (Fundamentals of Torah), discusses this. He talks about the possibility of somebody coming, after the giving of the Torah, and saying that he is also a prophet and that the Almighty told him to modify the Torah. We would say to him, "The Torah can never be changed, so how can we believe you?"

He might answer, "How can you believe Moshe Rabbeinu more than me? He was a prophet and I am a prophet."

We might then say, "We saw him perform so many miracles that our conclusion is that he could not be anything but a prophet."

The so-called prophet could answer and say, "I will also produce all kinds of miracles, and you will come to the conclusion that I am a prophet." Maybe as a sorcerer or black-magic kind of person he could perform some things.

At this point, the Rambam says, we would be in trouble. Therefore the Almighty says, "The fact that Moshe Rabbeinu was a prophet will not be known to you by witnessing proofs which he may perform, but rather by *experiencing prophecy together with him.*" When the Ten Commandments were given, everyone listened together with Moshe. Thus, everyone was a prophet at the same time, "in order that the people should hear when I am talking with you," and then belief in Moshe Rabbeinu's transmission would remain forever. Nobody would be able to take that away, because the nation could then say, "We also saw it, and we have this knowledge by experience and not by conclusion."

If someone will come along and say, "I am also like Moshe," we can say to him, "Fine. Maybe you are. But give us another experience like the Ten Commandments, the Giving of the Torah. We'll all be together with you, listening to what the Master of the World tells you."

This is the built-in safety mechanism that the Torah will stay with us and that nobody will be able to doctor it up. The experience that we shared with Moshe Rabbeinu gave us a belief in Moshe and in the Torah that will last forever.

THE PROPHETIC EXPERIENCE

Prophecy is not an easy thing. We can't weigh what it is, but we know that it is a communication from another world, which is a world that is not material at all, but only spiritual.

The Rambam explains that 613 *mitzvos* were given to Moshe from Sinai. The numerical value of the word "*Torah*" is 611. The first two we heard from the Almighty Himself, and the other 611 we heard from Moshe Rabbeinu. It was necessary to hear the first two from Hashem Himself so that we could later answer the false prophets who would claim they had received another Torah.

Then the Rambam explains why it was necessary to hear the 611 *mitzvos* from Moshe, rather than directly from Hashem.

He says that there are many different levels of prophecy. The greater a man is, the clearer is his prophecy. Of all the prophets in history, only Moshe Rabbeinu saw everything absolutely clearly. The other prophets saw through a reflection, an image. All the people standing at Sinai were not at the level of Moshe Rabbeinu, but they experienced the prophecy together with him. After the first two, they were so afraid of the awesomeness of the experience (the *gemara* says that they all *died* when Hashem spoke and had to be resurrected) that they said to Moshe Rabbeinu, "Enough. We will remember those two . . ." Thereafter, the prophecy came to Moshe Rabbeinu clearly, but for everyone else it came through a filter, through "thick clouds." That is why the Almighty said to Moshe, "The same Ten Commandments which I am giving to you, I am giving to the people through a filter." But in any case, they were prophets.

The Rambam says that a person has to be very, very great to attain prophecy, which is a communication with the Master of the World Himself. Even Moshe Rabbeinu could not see everything. Later, he asked the Almighty, "Please show me your glory." The Almighty answered him, "As long as a person is alive, he will not be able to see Me."

The Rambam says that when the prophets had their revelation, they were extremely affected. They were blasted completely out of their normal consciousness. Their entire bodies were knocked out and only their minds were left. If their prophecy would have come to them at the level of Moshe Rabbeinu's, they would have died. Their entire bodies were crushed because the body is what stands in the way of perceiving, and receiving, from the spiritual world. "I will come in a thick cloud . . . in order that the people should hear what I am saying to you."

All the prophets who came later perceived with a less clear vision than Moshe's, because they were further away from the source. The filter takes the non-physical revelation and filters it progressively more physically until it reaches here, with each level of reception dependent on the particular prophet's level. This is what Hashem means when he says that He will "come down to the people." It doesn't mean *up* and *down*. It means that the revelation will be through a filter.

We are physical beings and all our concepts are physical. The non-physical is much too strong for us. Whatever we have inside of us that is non-physical is the source of our physical life, and our truest life. But in order to be exposed to a higher level of the non-physical, a filter is required.

Then, after the prophet had his revelation and he came to the people, we were given ways of testing his prophecy to find out if he was a true or a false prophet. Nachmanides (the Ramban) says that even before his prophecy is tested, the greatness and honesty of the man should first be tested. If, after all that, he is accepted as a prophet, it is not because of any wonders that he performed, but because he passed the known tests of true prophecy.

THE DANCE AT THE WEDDING OF THE JEWISH PEOPLE

The Rambam says, in his *Letter to the Yemenites*, that the experience at Sinai was the dance at the wedding of the Jewish people. If someone wants to come and change the Torah, he will have to provide us with another wedding ceremony, says the Rambam. This will not be easy, to say the least.

When Moshe Rabbeinu came to the people in Egypt, he went first to the elders of the people. Before Joseph died, he had left word with his brothers to pass on to the people: "Someone is going to come and take you out from this country." He gave them a few signs with which they would be able to determine if the person was the true redeemer. Just as we have had in our history many people who came and called themselves Messiah and then turned out to be false, it could also have happened in Egypt. One of the signs Joseph gave them to look for was whether the redeemer would address the elders.

⌊§ (Rabbi Meir Abowitz *zt"l*, my father-in-law, said in one of his *sefarim* that this was because the elders understand better than the masses. If somebody has something good and true, which he means for the community's benefit, he goes to the elders. They understand more, and if the society is organized and sensible, they follow their elders. If the *elders* accept him, it may be good. But if somebody is a self-promoter, he would not go to the elders right away, because they will most likely catch on to him. Instead, he goes to the masses and creates a mass movement, and then he forces himself upon the elders.)

⌊§ In the days before the giving of the Torah, the Almighty was not talking directly with the people. Moshe Rabbeinu was the go-between, and he had been speaking to the elders. Then the people said, "We want to hear it from the Master of the World Himself." The Almighty said, "Fine."

When it started, it was like an earthquake and thunder, and like lava coming out of a mountain. It was a terrifying thing. The mountain was trembling. It says in *Hallel* that the mountains jumped like lambs, and the hills like sheep. The Rambam says that this is not a poetic image. That is exactly what happened. "The sea saw and ran away" is also not an image, but an actual experience.

All this happened before the people experienced the Ten Commandments.

They came to Moshe Rabbeinu and said, "This is too much for us. You take the Torah and you give it to us."

He said, "Nothing will happen to you." He quieted them down. Then they heard the first two commandments clearly. After that, they were again frightened, and with the other eight commandments they heard that Hashem was speaking to Moshe, but they couldn't understand what He was saying. They needed Moshe Rabbeinu to tell them.

Then they were afraid that the Almighty was going to give them the 613 *mitzvos* like this and that it was too much of an experience for them to take. So they came again, and they said, "The Ten Commandments are enough for us to hear. You bring the other 603 to us." And Moshe agreed.

But what they saw and experienced was enough to sustain their belief in Hashem, in Moshe, and in Torah, and to answer all the false prophets throughout the rest of history.

REVELATION TODAY

There is a great similarity between Avraham Avinu and Moshe Rabbeinu. Avraham, in his search for truth, went as far as he could humanly go. The *Midrash* says that he was like a man who passed by a beautiful building and stopped and admired it. He said, "Is it possible that such a structure does not have a manager?" So he sat there and tried to figure out who the manager was. Then somebody looked through the window and said, "Young man, I understand that you are looking for me. Let me introduce myself. I am the owner."

This is saying that when a person has exerted all his abilities, all his resources and capabilities, and he searches and comes to the last point, from which he can't go any further, then he deserves to receive an answer from, and be led directly by, the Almighty. *That* is revelation. To Avraham, Hashem said, "I am going to give you revelation because you have reached such a height that everything you can reach with your own mind, you have already reached. Now you need the answers by revelation."

Moshe Rabbeinu came to it in another way. He went as far as he possibly could to be honest. He was pasturing his sheep, and he tried to go away from any area where his sheep might go into someone else's property. He took them to the desert. This is an expression of great honesty. This led him as far as Mount Chorev, also known as Sinai.

There is a certain similarity between Avraham in intellectual research and Moshe in honest behavior: If a person goes as far as he can, then for the rest of what he needs, the Almighty picks him up and brings him further.

Today, we have revelation in the Torah. Hashem says, "If you will listen to My voice and guard My covenant, you will be to Me a treasure out of all the nations, because the entire world belongs to Me. You will be a kingdom of priests and a holy nation."

This is not a "reward," but rather an *opportunity*, and a promise. If a person gives someone else a business and says, "If you will work in that business, you will be a successful man," he doesn't give him a reward. He gives him an opportunity. In this case, it is an opportunity for a special closeness with the Master of the World.

ও How can we hear the voice of the Almighty? "Listen to My voice" refers to the Oral Law, which is where Hashem's voice is found. "Guarding My Covenant" comes about only through studying and observing the Oral Law. That is the guard for everything. Someone told me that one day in Palm Springs, California, there was a group conversion of twenty-six people from Judaism to Christianity. It's very tragic. Yet there is nothing to be surprised about. What did they know of their *Yiddishkeit* to prevent them from converting? Therefore, to *guard* means to *learn*.

Then "you will be My treasure." This means that then you will be special to the Almighty. When someone runs a business with many departments, they all work together, supporting each other, but there may be one special department which actually brings in the profits. For example, there may be an advertising department, a packaging department, and an invoice department — all of which are necessary. But without the sales department, they would all have nothing to do.

This is the idea of a "treasure out of all the nations." The Torah was created before the world was created. It is the blueprint for the whole of Creation, and the letters of Torah are the life and energy source for everything that exists. Hashem says, "Your job is to be in the switch room of the universe, listening to My voice and guarding My covenant. This is your place in the world. This is where your revelation is to be found."

◆§ In addition, there is more involved than our *own* revelation. The Jew in human society, whether we like it or not, is the little furnace which keeps a room heated. The furnace does not go out to take a walk in the room, or else it may set it on fire. But if you want to have a temperature of seventy degrees in the room, the furnace itself most likely needs to work up to a temperature of several hundred degrees. This means that it is not for the Jew to be a missionary. Our function is to be what we are supposed to be, and this is enough to keep the whole room warm. "Listen to My voice and guard My covenant," and the goodness will radiate out.

REVELATION IN EXILE AND IN PERSECUTION

When Moshe Rabbeinu had his revelation, the Chumash says, "An angel of Hashem appeared to him in a flame of fire, from the midst of the bush." There are all kinds of bushes, but this one was a *thornbush*. Rashi points out that there are so many beautiful plants and trees, but the Almighty chose to appear to Moshe Rabbeinu in a thornbush. This means, he says, that when the Jewish people are in exile and in trouble, the Almighty says, "I am with them." This is like someone who has a good friend who is in trouble. In that case, he wouldn't go to his friend dressed in his finest. Likewise, says the Almighty, "I appear in a thornbush."

◆§ Then it says that "Moshe saw that the bush was burning and was not consumed." From the very beginning, the Almighty showed Moshe Rabbeinu something about the Jewish people: They have no promise that they will not be tortured. They will be. But they have a promise that they will never be consumed.

The revelation and the promise have been with us throughout our history and are with us today, no matter where we are, and no matter under what conditions we are living.

⌐§ At the end of the Chumash, it says that the Torah is not in the heavens. In the *gemara*, it says that Rabbi Yehoshua and Rabbi Eliezer had a difference of opinion when they were learning in Yavneh with the Sages. A *bas kol* — a voice from Heaven — came out with a decision. Rabbi Yehoshua stood up and said, "It could be that this is a voice from Heaven, but we do not rule according to it because the Torah was given to us."

The quotation from the Chumash is: "It is not too hard for you, neither is it far off. It is not in the Heavens that you should say, 'Who shall go up for us to Heaven and bring it down to us and make us hear it that we may do it?' Neither is it beyond the sea that you should say, 'Who shall go over the sea and bring it to us and make us hear it that we may do it?' But the word is very close to you, in your mouth and in your heart that you may do it."

Idol Worship and the Denial of Revelation

The pagans don't care who the boss is. They care only about who can deliver the goods. That's why they have many different gods, but they never have a god who is the Creator.

WHAT IS IDOL WORSHIP?

A man goes into a department store. The owner is elsewhere, in his office. But there are clerks at the counters. There is one counter for perfumes, one for cameras, one for electrical appliances, and so on. The customer sees a camera that he wants, but it's very expensive — $2,000. He wants the camera, but he's not prepared to pay the price. So he calls the clerk aside and says, "Could you steal the camera for me? I'll pay you $120.00." It's a bargain.

This is what idol worship is. People imagine that there are so many things in this world to get that there must be some powers which are in control of each thing and are delegated to give them out. The person thinks that if he could only learn how to please that power, then what he wants will be given to him. Thus was created a god of love (Venus), a god of war (Mars), a god of success, of health, and many others. The pagans made copies of their images of those gods, and they served those copies. It's a combination of superstition and selfishness.

The man tries to bribe the god. Who cares about the boss? Who needs him? Who cares about a purpose for everything? The clerks can deliver the goods. Just pay them. The most important thing is who can deliver the goods at the cheapest price.

In this respect, there is no difference between the one who serves idols and the atheist. It's the same selfishness. Both of them care only for themselves and their own needs.

The idol worshiper is simply looking for something to serve him. The Chumash says, in relating Pharaoh's dream, "And Pharaoh was standing over the Nile ..." The *gemara* says that the Nile was worshiped by the Egyptians, because prosperity in Egypt depended upon the Nile. Since it gave them their needs, they worshiped it. This sentence from Chumash shows the relationship of Pharaoh with the Nile. He was "standing over it." The wicked are standing over their gods, because all they want is for their gods to serve them.

In contrast, when Yaakov Avinu had a dream, it is related thus: "And Hashem was standing over him." A *tzaddik* realizes that Hashem is over him.

ON PRAYING FOR OUR NEEDS

The very first thing to understand is the difference between Torah and idol worship.

The Jew is interested in more than the pagan is. The Jew is interested not only in what he *needs* and who can give it to him, but in who the owner is, and what his responsibilities to the owner are.

If we need something, we ask Hashem. We go straight to the Boss. But it's not enough to ask for something because we *need* it. As Jews, we have to realize that we *belong* to Him. Just as a soldier has obligations to the army which is supporting him, we have obligations to Hashem, who is supporting us.

If prayer's only purpose were to ask for our needs, it wouldn't be a *mitzvah*. The *mitzvah* is there because prayer reminds us of our dependence on Hashem. A person has to realize that everything he has comes from Hashem, and then he won't misuse it. That includes not only his livelihood and his material goods, but also his *capabilities*, such as his intelligence and reasoning abilities. It all comes from the Master of the World. The process of prayer is the process of growing in humility and submitting ourselves to the Sustainer of the World, which strengthens our *emunah*. Thus, it becomes a *mitzvah* to ask for our needs, in order to remind us that our success is not dependent on the work of our own hands.

⊷ The Jew doesn't ask for a blessing for his bread. He says, "Thank You, G-d, for giving me the bread." He's not asking G-d to serve him; he realizes that he has to be grateful to G-d for giving him this.

That is the difference between the giver and the taker. Idol worshipers are *takers*. A person would like to have everything, but there are some things which are not in his reach, so he conjures up a mysterious power that can give him whatever is beyond his reach.

Children are very much like this. They are concerned with who is going to bring them a gift and give them toys. A truly mature person is interested in more than simply receiving gifts. The realities of life teach him that if he wants to consume, he has to produce. Only the child thinks he can take and not give. He would like to have things, so he dreams that maybe there will be a miracle.

This is also superstition. The human being has a tendency to visualize the things that are beyond his understanding and conception as some kind of dark zone. He tells himself that maybe in that dark zone there is some power which he can call on and use.

The "mysticism" that is talked about today is a kind of idol worship. They talk about performing miracles with mysticism. They don't exactly understand how it works, but they say that over *there*, in that area, is a key to what they want. Many of those who teach Jewish mysticism have the same general misunderstanding of it. They think that Jewish mystics are some people who have found a key and keep it for themselves. "It's a good thing. Why should they give it to others?" If you search under the teachings of some of the most famous people who are teaching Jewish *Kabbalah* and mysticism, these ideas are at the root of their teachings.

THE GOLDEN CALF

In Chumash, in *sefer Devarim*, the nation is warned against the great dangers of idol worship. They had been exposed to the paganism of Egypt and the nations they were conquering on the east bank of the Jordan. They were now about to come into a land of paganism. They were warned not to go in those ways: "... lest there is among you a man, woman, family, or tribe whose heart turns away from Hashem." Also, "... lest there is among you a root which will one day produce bitter herbs."

When the Torah uses the term "turn away," it is referring to people who haven't yet gone very far away. If a person is going on a road and comes to a fork in the road, when he chooses one way and starts on it, initially the difference is very small — perhaps only one or two yards. But if he chooses the wrong road, then after some time he will be miles away from his goal.

This is what the Torah is talking about. "Maybe you have among you people who have a turn of heart, who didn't yet go too far, but whose hearts are worshiping idols. That root will one day produce bitter herbs."

The danger might have come about through the exposure the Jews had to idolatry. In Egypt they saw powerful displays of idol worship, and they might have thought that this was what gave the Egyptians their success. Even though later they saw that it was all broken down and destroyed, the memory of the beauty of those successful times might remain in their minds and hearts. "You might want to join or to imitate those idol worshipers."

The expressed reason for the sin of the Golden Calf was because Moshe had not come back in the time they calculated that he should have returned, and they wanted a leader. They had just come out of Egypt after 210 years of slavery. They had already become used to the idolatrous idea that there were some forces to which they could look, forces which would give them what they needed.

Moshe Rabbeinu had performed great miracles during the period before they left Egypt. Then suddenly he disappeared. So they said, "Maybe there's someone else who can give us what we need." So they said to Aharon, "Make us a god." However, the word they used, "elohim," doesn't mean "god." It means "a power." This idea, that there are different powers, had been learned in Egypt, the land of idol worship. So they said, "Moshe Rabbeinu delivered the goods, but he's not here. Let's get some other agent to deliver the goods." So they made a copy of an image, which was the Golden Calf.

↝ Even though they knew rationally that the miracles in Egypt had been performed by Hashem and not Moshe, it is not difficult to understand how they could now ascribe them to Moshe. The entire philosophy of idol worship is an off-balance thing. As long as people love themselves and want to get what they want, then they lose their balance.

In addition, they had also seen the paganism of the nations they conquered. They saw the promiscuity that accompanied idol worship. This was the root which left an image in their minds, and which would later produce bitter herbs.

If someone carries around in his head a longing for paganism, this will have a bitter ending. On a mass level, this can bring destruction to the people.

At the time of the Golden Calf, there were some people who wanted promiscuity, perhaps only on a subconscious level. They had seen it already, and that was enough to make the impression and enable them to fool themselves into thinking that they wanted a leader, when they really wanted promiscuity. Our Sages tell us that the underlying motivation for idolatry is actually promiscuity.

When Moshe Rabbeinu came down from the mountain with the Tablets in his hands and found the people celebrating around the Golden Calf, he threw the Tablets to the ground, shattering them. The idol worship of the people had taken the *life* out of the Torah they had received a short time before. Whatever they had received, and whatever Moshe Rabbeinu had learned during those forty days he was on the mountain, became an ineffective shell, with no life in it. The people no longer deserved to have the Torah at such a high level. Moshe had to go back up the mountain, where he was taught the Torah all over again. Finally, on Yom Kippur, the process was completed and the Jewish people were forgiven.

But the danger of entering into idol worship stood over them, threatening to take the life force out of Torah once again.

THE END OF IDOL WORSHIP

For the most part, we talk of idol worship among the Jewish people in the *past tense*. During the first *Beis Hamikdash* (Temple), there was idol worship. It involved important kings also, like Achav, Yeravam, and Menashe. Then, after the Babylonian exile when they came back to *Eretz Yisrael*, Ezra and the Men of the Great Assembly prayed that the inclination for idol worship among the Jewish people should be removed. They didn't have this inclination during the second *Beis Hamikdash*. They made other mistakes, but not idol worship.

On Succos, during the time of the second *Beis Hamikdash*, there was a tremendous celebration in the *Beis Hamikdash* called *simchas beis hasho'evah*, during which water was poured on the altar. They brought it from a spring in Jerusalem. The *Mishnah* has a beautiful description of the great *simcha* (rejoicing), during which every house in Jerusalem was lit up from the great light of the candles in the *Beis Hamikdash*.

There are several reasons for the celebration. One of them is that it was a celebration of the fact that there was no longer any desire for idol worship. They expressed special thanks for not having that temptation, which could have caused them to lose their most precious gift: the Torah itself.

IDOL WORSHIP TODAY:
THE MISUSE OF NATURAL FUNCTIONS

Holiness comes about when we live correctly with nature. This means that we have to search for and know exactly what the purpose is of that which we have, and to use it for that purpose. If you utilize whatever you were given for the purpose for which it was given, this is holiness. If we don't know what the purpose is for something, then we have to look for it in the Torah.

Historically, sexual promiscuity — the unbridled pursuit of personal pleasure — almost always accompanied idol worship. In fact, they were so tied together that the worship of the idol was often simply an attempt to legitimize what was really only a search for personal pleasure.

Today, society at large is in a state of great confusion and insecurity because all we are doing, on an individual and collective basis, is looking for the keys to happiness, convenience, and pleasure. It is not unlike the early idol worship, and it is equally dangerous.

THE KEY TO HAPPINESS

The real key to happiness, however, is found elsewhere. It consists of one very simple thing: Everything was created for a purpose. Use it for the purpose for which it was created, and you will be happy, and so will everyone else.

All of nature is one harmonious machine. If there is a need for something, many channels in nature work in harmony with each other to fulfill that need.

The way in which we relate to food is an example of forces of nature working in harmony. The purpose of food is to provide the energy that is needed for us to function. There are so many parts in the human body that work together. There are foods with all kinds of tastes, for example, in order to make the intake of food more pleasant. The sensation of hunger has also been provided. When we use energy, we feel hungry. The sensation of taste makes it easier to eat and to digest, while enabling us to distinguish between good food and spoiled food.

If one utilizes all those natural channels for the purpose of being healthy, then he is healthy. If he forgets the function and follows only his craving for taste, he winds up doing himself physical harm. So we see the principle of using things for their correct and natural purpose.

A person was given the ability to speak and to express himself. He was given this for some purpose. Perhaps the purpose is that whatever is born in his mind should not die together with him and disappear. The means of communication are there for a purpose. But if a person uses speech for slander and for lies, that's a misuse of nature and will certainly cause harm.

Both Torah and nature seem to indicate that one of the most important functions of the human being is to reproduce himself and bring more people into the world. Since it is such an important part of the human being, the very first *mitzvah* in the Torah is the *mitzvah* of reproduction.

According to the Torah, this is only a beginning. Thereafter, it is the parents' duty to raise the children to be useful people, which includes the obligations of establishing a home in which the children will be raised, of the parents being faithful to each other, of teaching the children Torah, and so on.

In order for a person to eat, he doesn't need anyone else. He only needs the means to buy his food. However, since another person is needed for the *mitzvah* of reproduction, we experience the force called *attraction*. The attraction of the sexes must be utilized for a person to find his mate, and it also helps to keep them together peacefully. The love that develops is also a natural part of this force which keeps them together.

The Torah's viewpoint is that since this is one of the most important functions of the human being, it should not be wasted. The more that people live up to the Torah's idea of the function of sex, the more happiness they will find. The more they do not live up to that function, the greater the unhappiness and disaster that will follow.

One cannot achieve happiness when he pursues happiness. If one pursues the pleasures of taste in food as an end in itself, he will eventually lose all appreciation of taste. If one is only after the pleasures of sex, he winds up destroying his own sexual pleasures.

Since modern life has gone off the track sexually, there are all kinds of illnesses and problems spreading in society. Great men have fallen short of achieving great things due to an absorption in this area. The *true* function has been lost, and endless social problems have followed in its wake.

The Torah says, "Be a holy people." Rashi asks, "What is holiness?" He answers by saying, "You attain holiness by staying away from a loose sexual life; by keeping this most important function sacred and not wasting it." Again, this is the idea of using what you have been given for its true function.

The Torah gives sex great consideration because it is one of the greatest aspects of the human structure. We must utilize more moral strength and more self-control to keep it on the normal track.

৵ In a natural home, as defined by the Torah, there is a lot of
happiness. In fact, the maximum pleasure is derived by founding a normal home. The antidote to idol worship today is to channel all our natural functions and gifts in the most productive manner, through the ways that the Torah shows us.

Marvels of Creation

THE EARTH AS OUR PANTRY

There is a well-known man in the Jewish community in London who is very unusual. He lives in a big house and it is open to guests. Anyone who comes to London can find a room to sleep and can go into the dining room and find food. I was visiting there once and went into the kitchen and found several tables with prepared desserts on them. Anyone was welcome to go in and take a dessert. He can also go to the refrigerator and the pantry and take food. In addition, the owner has a beis midrash in the house. You can go in and take a gemara and sit and learn. The house is unique in the whole world. I know of some people from Jerusalem who decided to take a vacation. They went to London and went to his house. They stayed there for a week or ten days and then came back.

Once a man needed to stay there for about three weeks, and he was feeling bad about it. He told the man with whom he was eating, "You know, I feel bad. I've been here for three weeks already, enjoying the hospitality, and I don't pay for anything." The other man said, "Don't feel bad. I've been here for years already."

It was the owner of the house himself!

Now imagine if the owner has to go away for three years. If it were just for a few months, he could bring in some more refrigerators and store food. But for three years, he can't do that. He wants to leave the house open and leave enough for all his guests for all that time. The only way he could do this would be to call in an inventor and tell him to do something to his walls so that the walls will produce food. A piece of cake from the wall . . .

◄§ This is exactly what the Creator did for us. The earth is our bedroom, our living room, and our kitchen, and it goes on producing fruit. Here you have an apple, here you have an orange, here you have a banana. It's wonderful!

The Master of the World has created everything for our needs, but that is not enough. If you have food, but you have no appetite, you'll starve. So He also gave us the will to eat, the appetite.

He enabled us to enjoy our food. Even if we wouldn't enjoy it, we would have to eat in order to exist. This is a special kindness of the Creator. Not only does He want us to exist, to sustain ourselves, but He wants us to enjoy it also.

◄§ There are those who point to countries where famine exists and say that this is a proof against the existence of the Creator. But we can perceive the correct perspective on this from the following analogy:

Suppose a man's wife does not know how to cook. Every day she feeds him canned goods. One day he's tired of this, so he goes to the market and buys a bag with all the best things. Steak, lamb chops, everything of the best quality. He takes the bag and puts it on the kitchen table and says, "My wife, let us have a good supper tonight."

He won't have it, because she doesn't know how to cook. She will ruin the ingredients.

That is what is happening to our society. We have been given all the ingredients, but we ruin it by selfishness and greed. If you go from country to country and try to find out how the country is being run, you find out how the country ruins itself.

There is a *midrash* which says that after Hashem created the first man, Adam HaRishon, He showed him around the garden. He said to Adam, "Look; what I have created is beautiful and perfect. My creatures are good and beautiful. Keep your mind straight; don't make mistakes and spoil My Creation."

We are the bad cooks. The Creation is good. *Man* makes the evil. We are told this by the prophet who says, "And you should know" — you should intellectually understand — "what is bad." See with your own eyes that when it is bad, it is also bitter.

We have been given all the ingredients to make it good.

THE ORIGIN OF THE JEWISH PEOPLE

There is a poem that some congregations say at the end of the Shabbos morning prayers: "They imagine You not as You actually are, but by considering Your deeds." This is saying that the only idea we can have of Hashem is through His actions. We have no concept of *essence*, only external *forms*. We know only what electricity can produce, for example. But we do not know what it *is*.

This is also saying that it is very hard to prove Hashem's existence and the Divine origin of Torah. But we can prove it indirectly. We can prove that *it couldn't be otherwise*.

There is a method in mathematics of proving things by demonstrating the alternative as an absurdity. Likewise, concerning belief in G-d, we can indirectly prove that anything else is an absurdity.

Some people say, "We can't believe in it. We don't *know*." The problem is that they don't try to think. If one tries to think, there are so many things that lead you up to the feeling that there's a Power that is handling everything.

Before Moshe Rabbeinu became the teacher of the Jewish people, he was given a test to see whether he was a person who wanted to understand things. He saw the bush burning, and he said, "Let me go aside and investigate why it does not become consumed." If a person is not curious, you cannot teach him anything. But the curiosity has to be not just to *know* what is going on, but to *understand* what is going on. Moshe Rabbeinu said, "I want to investigate *why* it is burning thus."

We can learn from this what an intelligent person is: When he sees things, he tries to understand them. An intelligent person looks at the world in order to understand what is behind it, and he comes to understand that somebody is managing everything.

As we have mentioned previously, there is a *midrash* that talks about the origin of the Jewish people: Avraham Avinu is compared to a man who saw a building. He stood outside it and he was wondering who the manager of the building was. While he was standing there, a window opened, and somebody looked out at him and said, "I think you are looking for me. I am the owner of this structure."

It is very interesting that Avraham didn't ask who the owner of the building was. He asked who the *manager* was.

A clue to understanding this is found in another *midrash* which talks about the first six days of Creation, up until the creation of man on the sixth day. The *midrash* says that up until that point, the story of the Creation is "Divine Glory." Don't try to decipher it. But from the point of the creation of man, the story of mankind is "Royal Glory" or "Royal Law." Research, and learn, and try to understand it.

"Royal Law" refers to the management of society and the rules of behavior and the rules of character. Avraham Avinu was looking for the manager because he wanted to know and to understand the rules of social behavior. He knew that if there is a manager and if you go according to his rules, society succeeds. If you don't go according to his rules, it fails. He wanted to know who the manager was.

But the one who opened the window to him — the Almighty — said, "It's much deeper than *managing*. You have to go further. It involves the entire nature of the Creation. You will do better to know Me as the Owner and Designer of the Creation, and then you'll understand the management also."

When Avraham Avinu exerted all his abilities and searched until the last point, he had his revelation and his proof.

This was the origin of the Jewish people: searching for the G-d Who is the Creator.

MARVELS OF CREATION

In the book of Koheles (Ecclesiastes) Shlomo Ha-melech discusses many theories of philosophy. But he doesn't touch on a discussion of a Creator at all. He discusses sense in life and happiness in life; does intelligence make you happier or unhappier? How to live and what to make of our lives is a topic for discussion. But he does not discuss whether there is a Creator or not. This is because it is so obvious to him that it is not even for discussion.

Rabbi Akiva makes the same point. He says, "If you see a house, you're convinced that there is a builder. If you see a garment, you're convinced that there is a tailor. And if you see a universe, you are convinced that Someone created it."

E very little part of Creation shows how much planning and how much art there is in it; so much perfection.

I was sitting in the waiting room at the dentist's office, and I saw a picture on the wall of human dentures. I studied the picture, and I discovered how perfectly they grow. The upper and the lower teeth grow so that they interlock. There is one upper between two lowers. One lower between two uppers. This is perfectly suited for the bite. If not, the bite wouldn't be right. Who planned this?

People don't want to observe. There is a very precise system in nature. I had to go to the dentist in order to find that out about teeth. But the entire human body is like this. Every function of the human body coordinates with every other function. The brain contributes to every part. There are so many systems that work together when a man raises his hand: the blood system, muscles, nerves, a command coming from the brain. Who gives the order? Who designed it?

The human body itself starts from a cell, which produces more cells, to produce more human beings. This is the miracle of human reproduction.

If a person would be born in a jungle, as he grew up he would look at the trees and the animals around him, and he would come to the conclusion that it's not just an accident.

Would anyone say that an automobile can be made by accident? That there was no engineer making it? No one would say that. But we are a thousand times more of a marvel than a car.

We are walking, marvelous machines, and anyone who imagines that it just *happened* is clearly not thinking.

If I simply think about a fruit and a tree, *that's* enough. How does a tree develop out of a little kernel? And the air and the soil share together in a partnership to create that tree. It's a marvel. I wouldn't know how to do it, and I don't know anyone who would know how to do it. Can anyone make a tree?

The most important thing is observation of the universe. The more I observe it, the more I marvel about it: the way an orange develops, protected by the skin, full of chambers inside protecting it. If you take a little part of that orange and plant it, you'll have a tree of oranges.

These days, computers are being used to demonstrate that Torah is Divinely given. Intricate codes in the Torah, far beyond the ability of a human being to devise, are being revealed by the computers. But I don't need that. If somebody would ask me what my proof is, I would say that a potato is my proof. All I have to do to believe in a Creator is to analyze a potato. A potato is a marvel. It's good in *cholent* also, but it's a marvel. We make a *berachah* before we eat it; the meaning of the *berachah* is that I am not just taking it, but that it is *given* to me. We are so used to taking things for granted that somebody could think that potatoes grow in *Machaneh Yehudah*, the open-air marketplace. How would he know otherwise? He goes over there and buys potatoes, so that's where they grow.

But how does a potato come to exist? We don't understand it. We put some seed in the ground, and after a while it will be a field of potatoes. It's not done by itself. It's been engineered. And I know that the One Who designed it is a good engineer.

I would not be surprised if the scientists could make a synthetic potato in the laboratory. It may be the most beautiful and best-tasting potato in the world. But one thing would not work. That potato is not going to produce another potato. A potato may be smarter than a human; the human takes the potato and makes a *cholent*, but the potato makes another potato. *The essence of the miracle of seed is a great secret, and seed — whether human, animal, or plant — is something of an endless existence.* The potato today is a great-great-great-grandchild of a potato which was a great-great-great-grandchild of a potato. So it's clear that the One Who invented the first potato placed within it an unlimited, almost eternal, capacity for reproducing itself.

My father zt"l wrote an essay on *emunah* (faith) in which he says that if not for our emotions, which blind us, we would all be believers in Hashem. He says that it's as logical as Rabbi Akiva's example of the building which testifies to the builder, and the garment which testifies to the tailor.

There is another demonstration of this. Suppose a document were found which had perfect handwriting and perfect grammar and syntax. In addition, the content was very deep and organized, and the more it was studied, the more depth was found in it. A group of scientists wanted to discover who had written that document. One of them said, "Nobody wrote it. There was an inkwell and a piece of paper on a table. A cat passed by and turned over the inkwell, and this document resulted." It doesn't make sense. Nothing perfect can be done unplanned. There must be a mind behind it. There are so many things like this in Creation. There must be some superior engineering in this. But some people say, "No. It just evolved from a fish. Or a monkey."

EVOLUTION

The tendency of a human being to want to live without discipline and without obligations is so strong that it brings about wishful thinking, like the theory of evolution. That is a theory which allows one to be clear of obligations and controls.

Evolution cannot be proven. It cannot be believed because it just doesn't make sense, even if you go back and you trace everything to one cell. That one cell has such a tremendous potential in it that out of that cell an entire world has developed. That first cell must have been a very smart one. But who invented it? Evolution cannot explain it. In fact, evolution leaves so many things unsolved. It's much more logical for me to say that something or somebody — smarter than I am — invented it. In fact, it's very logical to believe.

They talk of the question of the age of the universe, and they tell us it is millions of years old. Somebody gave an illustration which points out the fallacy of this: Suppose a man grew up in a jungle alone, and then he came into an inhabited country and saw people for the first time. He found people who were twenty years old. He observed how much a person grew in a year and found that the growth rate at that age might be one-tenth of an inch. They told him that when they were born they were tiny infants, and they showed him the size of a newborn infant. Judging by his observations, he is going to conclude that those people are at least five hundred years old, because if their speed of growth is one-tenth of an inch a year and they were five feet tall, it would come out to over five hundred years.

The only problem is that he did not realize that the speed of growth is different at a younger age than at a mature age.

How do we know that at the time of the Creation of the universe it was developing at the same slow speed which we see today?

∾ The Chafetz Chaim's observation about the events of history speeding up in the period prior to Mashiach is a demonstration of this. We are seeing that now. We are witnessing that history does not always develop at the same speed. It's possible that at the time of Creation, it also developed at a very rapid rate.

Nobody can say for certain. The best anybody can do is come up with a theory. Theories which cannot be taken into the laboratory have not much value. Where is the laboratory for history? Where is the laboratory for the theory of evolution? There isn't any. So therefore history can have all kinds of wild theories.

Even though it is called the "theory" of evolution, if you talk to the teachers in the classrooms, they believe it as *fact*. But they have no laboratory. They have some fossils, but they have only theories to place dates on those fossils.

How did these theories come to be so widely accepted as fact?

In America, the principle of separation of state and church is very necessary. However, due to that, you cannot teach Creation in the schools. So therefore, the theory of evolution became the official philosophy.

∾ People tend to copy each other. A great part of our criteria is what is being accepted by other people. This is why a person born in a jungle wouldn't have that theory worked into his mind and would automatically draw the conclusion, based on his observations, that this is not all just an accident, but that there is some kind of a plan behind everything.

There are those who believe that the marvelous orange — its growth, development, and taste — came into being by itself. Can there be another reason for accepting that, other than that it seems that others accept it? This is the principle behind Madison Avenue advertising.

We have another laboratory, better than the classroom: "Just as the house testifies to the builder and the garment to the tailor, so the world testifies to the Creator."

Then, as soon as you have the principle of the Creator of the world, you have almost everything else as well.

There is also a laboratory of Torah and Jewish behavior. It says in Chumash, "Do not add anything to that which I command you, and do not take anything away from it." Do it exactly as you were told. Moshe Rabbeinu was speaking to the second generation in the desert, the generation that was coming into *Eretz Yisrael*, in the very beginning of the Torah portion of *Va'eschanan*. He says, "Your eyes have seen what Hashem did to all the people who followed that idol. Each and every one who followed that idol disappeared from your people. And you who cling to the Word of Hashem are all alive today." This pattern has continued throughout Jewish history, and this has been our laboratory that has shown us the truth and effectiveness of Torah.

Then you can understand that the Torah is of Divine origin. Just as investigation into the wonders of nature brings you to recognize the Creator of the World, awareness of the wonders in Torah, which are so great that they couldn't be human, brings you to know that Torah is Divinely given.

But in order to know this, you have to investigate Torah, to learn Torah. And the more you learn, the more you know for sure ...

Providence

The key to understanding everything that is happening to us is the understanding of the basic principle of Jewish history. Jewish history does not move on natural, normal tracks. Jewish history is moved by Providence.

Everything in Jewish history is planned and leads up to something.

WORLD HISTORY

The Chafetz Chaim *zt"l* said in 1913, one year before the First World War broke out, that the world at that time was coming close to the time of the arrival of Mashiach. Humanity had a number of unsettled accounts, he explained, and they would have to be settled fast. He mentioned that the *gemara* compares history to a turning wheel, and that from that time on, the wheel would start spinning fast and would keep on spinning faster and faster. International changes which used to take centuries would now occur in a span of months.

It's happening now. It started right after World War I. We saw it start in Versailles. So many countries were created overnight. The prewar world and the postwar world were two totally different worlds. The wheel slowed down between 1922 and 1939, and then in 1939 everything turned around. Since World War II, it's moving even faster. The changes in the way of life of society are tremendous. What we have witnessed in the past twenty years of

American society is a terrible spinning. This is all what the Chafetz Chaim talked about.

Some years prior to the Chafetz Chaim's prediction, the Malbim made a calculation, based upon the Book of *Daniel*, that the era of the coming of the Mashiach would start in 1913. But he didn't say how long that era would take. He said only that it would start then.

What happened in Russia is an example of the speed at which changes are taking place today. Communism came in promising to bring freedom and equality to all people, but it brought slavery and poverty. A few people were holding the reins in their hands. The Russian writer Solzhenitsyn wrote about life in Siberia. From his books it is possible to see what a strong organization they had. It was like an iron building. It was impossible to imagine that this would break down.

In his book, *Go My Son*, Chaim Shapiro also tells of his experiences in Russia — the control, the terror.

Then, suddenly, just as we pray on Rosh Hashanah and Yom Kippur that all wickedness should disappear like smoke, it happened. A natural event is when something which is powerful slowly begins to lose power and becomes weaker and weaker until it dies. But if, during a stage of full power, it suddenly turns around and becomes nothing — this is a miracle, the miracle of history speeding up in order to settle accounts.

We need to learn the right lessons from the events of history. If a person doesn't learn lessons and goes only by his own natural reactions, then the events in the Communist world are simply something that happened, without any meaning or substance.

A *talmid chacham* is referred to as a "learned person." But really, he is a *learning* person. This is what a Jew is. A Jew is always learning. If we learn the lessons, then we learn a lot and we grow a lot.

PROVIDENCE, EMUNAH, AND BITACHON

*E*munah, faith, is when we realize and are conscious of the fact that there is a Boss. He created us and we are responsible to Him. He put us here for a purpose.

◆§ In the *gemara*, in *mesechta Megillah*, it says that the students of Rabbi Shimon bar Yochai asked about the story of Esther, which we read on Purim. They wanted to know why the Jewish people deserved to experience such a terrible period, during which they were afraid that they were all going to be destroyed.

Rabbi Shimon asked them what *they* thought. They answered that it was because the Jews had taken part in the feast of Achashverosh. Rabbi Shimon answered that this was only a mistake of the people of Shushan, the capital, who actually attended the feast. But why were all the Jewish people in the empire threatened? There must have been another reason which would explain why the entire nation was threatened, and Rabbi Shimon went on to point it out to his students.

It was originally hard for me to understand what the students were looking for in their question to Rabbi Shimon bar Yochai. It says explicitly in the *Megillah* why Haman was angry: Mordechai did not bow to Haman, and therefore Haman became angry and wanted to destroy the whole nation. Why were the students looking for other misdeeds? The answer is that the *gemara* understands that what is happening internationally to the Jewish people is a kind of puppet show. Only a child looks at the puppets and thinks they are very smart and that they are such good dancers. But anybody who knows what's going on knows that the dancers are simply puppets. Somebody is pulling the strings.

◆§ The Ramban says that everything that happens to the Jewish people is Divine Providence. But Hashem does not do it openly. He handles the puppets. Rabbi Shimon bar Yochai's students were asking what was behind it. This is part of *emunah* — to realize that everything that is happening to us is by Divine Providence. Everything is happening through puppets.

The Torah wants us to look at all the situations that we as a people face, and to see that all those who come against us are puppets. Somebody is utilizing them for a purpose. It's not *them* that we essentially have to deal with. It is the *Master of the World* that we have to deal with.

◆§ When Moshe Rabbeinu sent the spies into *Eretz Yisrael* to search out the land before the Jewish people came in, their mistake was that they didn't look beyond the puppet show.

The spies came back and gave their report to the nation. On the surface, their initial report was very positive. But there was one word missing there. The Name of Hashem is never mentioned. Then they said, "It is a land that destroys its inhabitants." Rashi explains that wherever they went there were funerals, so they concluded that it was a terrible land. However, Rashi continues, the funerals were for their *benefit*, in order to keep the people busy so that they would not notice the strangers in their midst, spying out the land. So, for their protection, Hashem made it happen that the people were busy with their burials. But in the report the spies brought back, they were looking at everything without looking to the Almighty. And without that, all you see is the land killing its inhabitants. Wherever you go, there are funerals. Joshua also sent spies into the land. But his spies came back and told him the miracles that had happened to them: how they were chased, how they were not caught, and so on. They said, "Hashem has put this land in our hands. If this is what happened to two people, it is surely what will happen to the entire nation. Here is how Providence is guiding us."

◆§ If you want to judge Jewish history or foretell Jewish history, don't look at the political climate. Jewish history has nothing to do with the political climate. You have to look at the Divine climate. What is Providence doing? In what direction does Providence direct us? *Then* you can see. If Moshe Rabbeinu's spies would have looked at it in that way, they would have said, "If miracles happened for us, only twelve people, then look what kind of miracles will happen for 600,000 people!"

◆§ Today, we don't see the hand of Providence clearly. But if not for the hand of Providence, we are lost. By all natural laws, we are lost. But in fact, we are not. Through *emunah*, we realize that there is a Creator who created us. He put us here for a function, and we are responsible to Him. We live our *emunah* when we realize that the entire international situation is really a matter of the Master of the World pulling the strings. The puppets are dancing, singing, fighting, and performing.

◆§ *Bitachon* (trust) is when we understand not only that the Master of the World is pulling the strings and making them perform, but that He will straighten out everything. After we have applied all our *emunah* to understand Providence and all our skills to become at peace with the Boss, and we realize that with all this we still need Him to help us, then *this* is *bitachon*.

EMUNAH, BITACHON, AND JEWISH HISTORY

*B*itachon is also when we become grateful not only for being taken *out* of Egypt, but also for being brought *into* Egypt.

We had the privilege that Yaakov Avinu and his children came into Egypt and went through terrible times there. This doesn't make sense unless we understand that the time we spent in Egypt served a certain purpose.

ﱠ A child once asked a certain rabbi, "Why are we so grateful for being taken out of Egypt? Who put us there in the first place?"

It's a serious question, and the answer starts in the Haggadah. "Blessed is the One Who keeps His promise to Israel . . . The Holy One, Blessed is He, has calculated the date of carrying out his promise to Avraham Avinu in the Covenant Between the Parts." He said to Avraham Avinu at that time, "You should know that your children will be strangers in a land that does not belong to them. They will be enslaved and they will be tortured . . . It will take four hundred years. I will judge the people who enslave them, and after this they will come out with great wealth."

ﱠ This, in a nutshell, is the entire history of the Jewish people. Here will be found the sense — the reason — for the history of the Jewish people.

Normal history is a result of cause and effect. Jewish history is different. Since modern Jews often want to be a "nation like other nations," some historians try to write Jewish history in the same way as it is written for other nations. But this is not Jewish, because Jewish history does not occur by natural cause and effect, but by Providence. Our history does not move according to the same principles as the history of the rest of society.

We testify to this every day when we say, "*Shema Yisrael, Hashem Elokeinu, Hashem Echad.*" There are two different names for the Almighty in this sentence: *Hashem* and *Elokeinu. Elokim* means a master, a judge. We say, "*Elokei Avraham, Elokei Yitzchak, Elokei Yaakov.*" When we say "Master," it is in relation to something else. But the name *Hashem* means "*was, is, and will be.*" It is the most abstract expression for the name of the Almighty because it refers to eternal, self-sufficient being. A master is not self-sufficient, because he needs someone to be a master over. But the idea of an eternal being is an idea of self-sufficiency.

Elokeinu means "our Master." This means that there is a special relationship between the Almighty and the Jewish people. One might think that since there is a special relationship between ourselves and the Almighty, and we are His children — as it is written, "You are His children" — then everybody else has no relationship.

But this is not so. The same *Hashem* Who has a special relationship with us is *Echad*. He is One for everybody. He has a special relationship with us, but He has a relationship with the entire society. "You will be a special nation to Me out of the nations, for all the earth is Mine." That is to say, "All the nations belong to Me, but you will be My treasure." Your history will not be like their history.

◆§ Why were we sent into slavery in Egypt? What is it in our relationship with the Almighty that enables us to have gratitude for something that seems so terrible?

The *gemara* explains that Moshe Rabbeinu asked the same question. He said to Hashem, "Please show me Your glory." Sometimes we don't see the glory of Hashem. We see things happening, and we say, "How can He permit it?" The Almighty answered him, "As long as you are alive, you cannot have the answer."

That is also the same question that the Book of *Koheles* discusses when it says, "What benefit does a person have from all his labor under the sun?" The *gemara* says, "Under the sun there is no benefit, but above the sun, there is a benefit." The example of the aviator's clock is an analogy which helps to explain this: In the early days of aviation there were clocks which were designed for aviators to see. The clock had its workings in a room on the top floor of a building, and the face and hands were outside on the roof. If you stood in that room and tried to figure out what all that machinery was for, you would be perplexed — a lever moves a wheel, the wheel moves another wheel, that wheel moves a gear, and so on. It all seems so pointless. Only when you go *above* the roof do you see what it is all leading to. We don't necessarily have to know what everything means at every stage. This is *emunah* and *bitachon*.

There is a beautiful Chassidic story about this:

> There was a great *Rebbe* by the name of Reb Elimelech who lived at the time of the Czar's oppressive regime. The government was not friendly to the Jews, and from time to time they came out with all kinds of anti-Jewish regulations. The Chassidim always came to Reb Elimelech, and he always prayed that the regulations would not be carried out. His prayers were accepted, and during his lifetime there were no persecutions in his part of Russia. After he passed away, persecutions began. The Chassidim wondered about that, because it is written that *tzaddikim* are more powerful after their death than in their lifetime. Why were there more persecutions *after* his death than before?
>
> A group of Chassidim went to his grave and prayed for an answer. The next night, one of the Chassidim saw the *Rebbe* in a dream. The *Rebbe* said to him, "You and your friends came to my grave, and you want me to pray for you. I cannot do so; as long as I was with you and I saw something bad coming, I prayed for it to be annulled, and my prayers were accepted. But now that I am over here and I can see that *in fact it is not bad*, I cannot pray anymore. *You* have to pray."

There is another story which also illustrates the concepts of *emunah* and *bitachon* in the face of the most difficult circumstances. This story is told in the book of my father's life.

> A young Orthodox yeshiva student was in the American army during the Second World War and

was present during the liberation of the camps. Among the survivors who had originally come from Lithuania was a man who had been with my father zt"l in the last few days before he was killed. He approached the American soldier and related a parable that my father had told in those last days in response to a question about the meaning of the inferno of suffering which they were experiencing.

A man who knew nothing at all about agriculture came to a farmer and asked to be taught about farming. The farmer takes him out to a field and begins plowing. "Why are you tearing up a beautiful field?" cries the city man in surprise. The farmer does not answer. The farmer takes a bag of ripe grain and begins throwing it into the furrows of the field. "You are wasting good grain!" exclaims the amazed onlooker. The farmer then proceeds to water the field. "Why are you pouring water onto the ground?" The farmer is still silent.

After a few months shoots appear above ground, and soon there is a field of wheat. "Now I think I am beginning to understand," says the city man, only to be further confused when the farmer cuts down the entire crop. "Why all that work if you now destroy it?" Still no explanation. Then the wheat is taken to a mill and ground, and then, even more confusing, half of the ground grain is thrown to the wind — seemingly complete wastage.

The result of all this work is some fine white powder which the farmer takes home and proceeds to mix into a thick paste with water. The city man watches, perplexed, as the farmer shapes loaves and prepares to put them into his oven. "This is too much!" he cries in disbelief. "Now you are going to burn it!"

If the man from the city would leave at that point, he would never understand the process he has witnessed. It would forever seem like a process of senseless destruction. But if he remains until the fresh, steaming bread appears, everything will make sense. The entire process, each and every step, will be revealed as essential and constructive.

We are standing on this side of the furnace; we see only a process of pain and destruction. But we have the faith to know that on the other side, it will all be clear.

Hashem says, "My ways are not your ways. My thinking is not your thinking." With our thinking, we just don't understand it. But there is a higher thinking, and we have to live with the fact that we don't know. We just don't know.

THE LESSONS IN EMUNAH LEARNED IN EGYPT

Where is the hand of Providence? If somebody believes, he sees. But if somebody doesn't believe, he doesn't see.

We read in the *Haggadah*, "If He had not brought forth our ancestors . . ." If children would celebrate the anniversary of their parents' wedding, it would make sense. If those parents had not wed, the children would not have come into this world. So therefore, it's not only an event for the parents, it's also the children's event!

But would it also be important that the children go over the menu that was served at the wedding? It's not important whether there was fish or poultry. The important thing is that the parents are married.

It's the same thing with the events at the exodus from Egypt. We are grateful that we left there. But why are we commanded so strongly to tell over, at such great length, all the details?

We learn from this that this is not only a series of events that happened in that generation, but that they also happened to us and have an effect on our lives today.

The Ramban, in his discussion of the Torah portion *Bo*, says that one of the reasons why the Torah discusses in such detail so many of the events of the exodus from Egypt is that at that time the fundamentals of *emunah* were demonstrated.

First of all, the existence of Hashem and His power were visibly and powerfully demonstrated. It was demonstrated that the world does not function like a machine that was created to run by itself. The Master of the World is in control.

Hashgachah — that He has a concern with what is going on — was also demonstrated, as was *nevuah* — prophecy. When Moshe Rabbeinu said something, it happened exactly the way he said it would.

The Ramban says that these fundamentals are essential and that they were demonstrated so dramatically at the time of our very formation as a nation so that we should always remember them. We should learn the lessons of *emunah* from the miracles and wonders that accompanied our leaving Egypt.

"In every generation, a person is obligated to see himself as if he went out of *Mitzraim*," as if he had personally experienced the entire process of going out of *Mitzraim*. We should be grateful for it. For that, it is enough to know that there was a wedding. Also, we should learn lessons from it. In order to learn a lesson, we should know what happened at the wedding.

THE PROMISE

"And that promise stood for our ancestors and for us." In every generation, there are people who want to exterminate us, but the promise that we will always survive carries us through. This was not only a promise given for *Mitzraim*, but for the entire duration of the life of the Jewish people, until we will *come out* — until Mashiach comes.

Moshe Rabbeinu was told by the Almighty, "In the presence of your entire people, I will do wonders which have never happened to the earth or to any nation. The people whom you are among will see the works of the Master of the World. How awesome it is, what I am going to do with you."

This was not only told to the generation of the desert. It was told also for *us*, for every generation. In every generation, the people who are with Moshe Rabbeinu — the people who are learning and observing Torah — can recognize that there is nothing natural happening to the Jewish people. There are many things happening, especially today, that show us that these are not natural events. But who sees it? The people who have Moshe Rabbeinu in their midst — the people who are keeping Torah — see the acts of Hashem.

SONG OF SONGS AND THE HISTORY
OF THE JEWISH PEOPLE

In *Shir HaShirim* (Song of Songs), there is a verse which says, *"Mashgiach min hachalonos* — He watches through the windows; *meitzitz min ha'charakim* — He is peeking through the cracks (in the wall)."

A certain Chassidic *Rebbe*, in explaining this verse, said that if you sit in a room and somebody looks in from the window, he sees you and you see him. But if you sit in a room and someone peeks through a crack in the wall, he sees you, but you don't see him.

The *Rebbe* said that the same is true of the Providence which the Jewish people experience. Sometimes Hashem looks in through the window. He watches us, and we see that He is watching us. At other times, we don't think He is watching us. He looks in through the cracks in the wall.

But He always watches us.

Moshe Rabbeinu asked the Almighty, "Why did You send me to Pharaoh? It has become *worse* since I went." After the first confrontation with Pharaoh, he had increased the work load for the Jews. The Almighty answered, "*Now* you will see. Until now I was looking through the crack. So until now you had all kinds of questions. But from now on, I'll be at the window."

This lesson of the history of the Jewish people is also found in *Megillas Esther*. Rashi says that everything that is found in the Books of Prophets and Writings has to be found in the Chumash. The *gemara* asks, "Where is Esther in the Chumash?" It answers that a reference to Esther is found in the Book of *Devarim*, in chapter 31, verse 18. Just before this, it says, "Hashem said to Moshe: 'You are going to join your ancestors in the next world. After you have passed on, the people will err and follow the idols of the land ... I will become angry with them ... I will hide My face from them ... All kinds of troubles will meet them, and they will say that it is because Hashem is not with them.' I will hide My face... *V'anochi haster astir panai.*"

It is almost the same word as "Esther" — *hastir, astir.* The *gemara* says that this is where Esther is found in the Chumash. Throughout the Book of Esther, Hashem's name is never mentioned. Everything seems like a natural event, until at the end everything adds up, and the order of all the events together shows you that there was a plan behind it. Hashem says, "*Hastir astir panai* ... I will hide My face. I will see you. I will look and supervise. I will watch you through a crack in the wall, and you will not see Me.

But I will always be watching."

Miracles and Wonders

MIRACLES: HIDDEN AND REVEALED

A miracle demonstrates the existence of a higher Power.

"*Hastir, astir*" in the Chumash as a reference to Esther is not just a play on words. It points up for us an important element of the *Megillah*. The *mitzvah* of reading the *Megillah* is very important, and it is important to do so in a place where there is a large crowd, if at all possible. This is because part of the *mitzvah* of reading the *Megillah* is *pirsumei nissa*, publicizing the miracle. Being with a larger crowd gives more publicity than a smaller crowd.

When we are talking about the *Megillah*, we are talking about miracles. But where is the miracle? If you read the *Megillah*, there is nothing to be seen there but very simple and normal things. Nothing surprising. Achashverosh is drunk and kills his wife Vashti. That happens. It's known to happen. Then he misses his wife and looks for a beautiful wife replacement, and he picks out a beautiful girl who happens to be Jewish. This is also normal.

He has an anti-Semitic advisor and gives him a high position. There's nothing more normal than that. The anti-Semite gets piqued because someone does not greet him properly, and he wants to destroy the Jewish people. We're used to it.

Where are the miracles here? There is nothing supernatural in the entire story. So why do we call it a *nes*, a miracle?

∾ There are two possible ways in which a miracle can demonstrate the existence of a higher Power. One is where the miracle is clearly seen, and it doesn't require any reasoning to know that a miracle has occurred. In the story of Chanukah, there was a flask of oil which was supposed to last for one day, and it lasted for eight days. There is nothing to think about or understand. They saw with their eyes that something supernatural had happened.

It was the same with the miracles that came before we left Egypt. Suddenly the entire country of Egypt was darkened, and it was dark for a few days. It was a clear demonstration of the presence of a higher reality.

But sometimes there are demonstrations which we have to think into and understand, and then we come to the conclusion that they demonstrate a higher Power. We don't have to go far. We only have to look at the human body and the miracle of the engineering of it; how it reproduces itself, and how out of nothing a human being comes into the world. Is there any engineer or any scientist who can duplicate it? It's a demonstration of a higher Power.

But we don't think about it because we take it for granted. We see it day after day, and we don't question it.

When I was a child, when an eclipse of the sun occurred, we would observe it through dark glass. We used to take pieces of glass and hold them over a kerosene lamp to cover them with smoke. Then we would run to look through the smoky glass to see the sun. We would ask each other, "What makes the sun dark?" But we never discussed what makes the sun shine. We took for granted what we saw. When something unusual happened — the sun becoming dark — then we questioned it.

But the world around us is full of miracles. It is full of demonstrations of a higher Power.

The miracle in the *Megillah* is the *order* in which things happened. Esther became queen before Haman became powerful. It was a case of Hashem providing the cure before the illness. If it would have happened the other way around, it would have been a tragedy.

First, a Jewish girl had to be put into the palace. How could this be done? There was already a queen there, so something had to happen to the queen. The king had to get drunk and kill his wife.

It says in the *Megillah: "After all these things happened,* the king raised up Haman ..." All these things that had to happen — the feast of Achashverosh, the killing of Vashti, the looking for a wife, the finding of Esther — were all the conditions which led to the outcome.

Therefore, there was no supernatural event, but the order of all the events together shows you that there was a plan behind it. *There was not one miracle in the entire Megillah. But the entire Megillah is one great miracle.* Whatever happened in the *Megillah* was all by the supervision of the Master of the World. That's why there is a *halachah* that you have to read the *Megillah* in exactly the same order as it is written, because the entire miracle is the *order* of the events. This is a covered-up miracle.

The reason for the importance of publicizing the miracle is that a person may forget about it and think it "just happened." It just happened that Achashverosh killed his wife, that he fell in love with a Jewish girl ... It all just happened.

No. *Pirsumei nissa* — publicizing the miracle — reminds us that it is all planned. Hashem has a special concern about what happens to His people. We have a tendency to forget, but if we learn the lessons from the events — and tell them over repeatedly — we remember at all times. This is also what is involved in our repetition of the miracles at the time of the exodus from Egypt.

◁§ The same is true with current events. If we try to understand them, we can also find something of meaning. This is especially true after the events happen. If we start thinking of the events of the last hundred years, we can find a sequence that was leading up to something. This is also proof that Somebody is planning everything.

I read a newspaper not to know what happened today, but to know what I can expect tomorrow.

"MIRACLES" AND "WONDERS"

In the *Shemoneh Esrei* (eighteen-blessing prayer) which we pray three times a day, we say, "We thank You"; and among other things, "We thank You for Your miracles which are with us every day; and for Your wonders, for Your wonderful things. And for Your goodness which is with us always; nighttime, morning, and afternoon." We talk of *miracles* and we talk of *wonders*.

There is a story which illustrates the difference.

> Rabbi Chanina ben Dosa was a very great man, and extremely poor. The *gemara* says that he didn't have bread to eat all week; only carobs. On Shabbos, he would have bread.
>
> One day a tragedy occurred. He came into his house one *erev* Shabbos, Friday afternoon, and he saw that his daughter was upset. She had been preparing the candles for Shabbos, and instead of pouring in oil, she had poured in vinegar. For people of such great poverty, it was a tragedy.
>
> Reb Chanina ben Dosa asked her, "Why are you crying?"
>
> She told him about the vinegar in the candles.
>
> He told her, "If Hashem wants, vinegar will also burn. Try it."
>
> So she tried it and it burned.

The logic of Rabbi Chanina ben Dosa is very strong. We don't know why oil burns, and we don't know why vinegar doesn't burn. But we don't question the things to which we are accustomed. This is the difference between a miracle and a wonder. When oil burns, it is a wonder. When vinegar burns, it is a miracle because that is the thing which is unusual. In truth, we can't explain either one. But one — the oil that normally burns — we call a *wonder*, when we think into it. The other — the vinegar that suddenly burns — doesn't require any thinking into it, and we call it a *miracle*.

MIRACLES TODAY AND BELIEF

There are people who say they find it hard to believe because they don't see any miracles today.

> There is a story that is told about Rabbi Yisrael Salanter. An assimilated Jew in Vilna, whose daughter

was an accomplished dancer, once said to him, "We are always telling stories about miracles that happened thousands of years ago. Why don't we see any miracles today?"

Reb Yisrael did not answer immediately but waited until the man began bragging about his daughter and her dancing. Reb Yisrael then said, "I can't believe that your daughter knows how to dance."

The man said, "*Rebbe*, I'm telling you the truth."

"You know what," Reb Yisrael said, "if you want me to believe it, let her come and dance for me."

So the man said to his daughter, "Daughter, I want you to dance for the Rabbi."

She said, "Why?"

The father said, "The Rabbi doesn't believe that you know how to dance."

She replied indignantly, "I should dance because the Rabbi doesn't believe I know how to dance? If he wants to know, let him take a look at my diploma! I'm certainly not going to dance just for him."

Reb Yisrael said to the man: "What do you want? The Holy One, Blessed is He, should come dancing in Vilna because there's one unbeliever who doesn't believe that He can perform miracles?"

◆§ The Boss is around. Through the lessons we learn from being shown His wonders and miracles, He shows us that He is around.

Assimilation

It is written that the Almighty remembers the sins of the fathers for four generations, and that He remembers their kindness for two thousand generations. After four generations, people who have left Torah are no longer Jews. There is no one left to punish.

Here, in the beis midrash where we learn, we enjoy our lives. Once I was addressing the students in our yeshiva, Ohr Elchanan. The beis midrash then was very small, and people were crowded in. I told them I knew another place which was very crowded: Noah's Ark. All the animals in Creation were in the Ark, and it must have been very crowded. But I never heard it said that there were any complaints.

I know why they didn't complain. When there is a flood outside, you are grateful to be inside.

ASSIMILATION IN HISTORY

In Germany there was a great deal of assimilation and a great deal of intermarriage. For a while the assimilated Jew felt that he was fully German, and he tried to forget that he was a Jew. Hitler came and reminded him in the most cruel way. He dug out people who had not been Jewish for three and four generations.

Before assimilation happened in Germany, it happened in France. Until the French Revolution, the Jews all over the world were treated as strangers. They were kept in ghettos, abused in every way, and treated as people who had no rights. That came about, for the most part, in the Middle Ages, through the Church. There were also periods when Islam persecuted them.

Then the French Revolution came and broke the ghettos open. Many average Jews who did not have a strong hold on their ideals as Jews became drunk with that freedom. Similar to an explosion after pressure, they turned the other way and assimilated. After they came to feel that they were Frenchmen and nothing else, the Dreyfus affair occurred and showed them that they were still Jews.

In earlier days, close to two thousand years ago, there were also assimilationists. These were the Hellenists. But in the Middle Ages, large-scale assimilation didn't start until the French Revolution in the late 1700's. Then the old standards of the Jewish community eroded very rapidly.

> There is a story in the *midrash* about a Roman governor who was talking to Rabbi Yehoshua ben Chananya. The Roman said: "I am better than your teacher Moses. King Solomon said, 'A live dog is better than a dead lion.' Moses died a long time ago and I am alive, so I am more important."
>
> Rabbi Yehoshua said to him, "Let's try an experiment. You issue a decree that in three days from now nobody should make a fire. We'll see whether people obey you or not."
>
> On the third day they went out to the Roman's roof garden. They saw that from some chimneys smoke was rising.
>
> Rabbi Yehoshua said to him, "Look. My dead lion decreed long ago that a Jew shouldn't make a fire in his house on a certain day of the week — the Shabbos. There are no transgressions. You issued a decree three days ago, and people don't keep it. It seems that my lion is more alive than you."

If Rabbi Yehoshua could make a statement at that point in history that no Jewish person ever made a fire on Shabbos, we can see that the standards of the Jewish community were different than they are today.

At the time of the Second Commonwealth, there were some people who did not accept Torah entirely. They were the Sadducees. They claimed that they accepted the Written Law, but not the Oral Law. However, the Written Law without the Oral Law is of little use.

The Rambam says that in any case they were lying — they didn't believe in either one. The people would have stoned them if they had come right out and said they were non-believers. So they had to pretend that they believed. They lost nothing with their lying, because as soon as you are free to give your own interpretations to the law, you have full freedom to do whatever you want to do. You can always find an interpretation which will suit your convenience — "I, live up to the 613 commandments. How? My way. My interpretation."

This is very typical of many groups in the Jewish world today who are trying to give their own interpretations. They do it their own way and it becomes another religion.

I heard the story of a boy who was going to have a *bar mitzvah;* the grandfather had a little tradition in his background and wanted the boy to put on *tefillin*, at least on the day of his *bar mitzvah*. The rabbi wouldn't hear of it. "He'll have a big ceremony. The mother will take out the Torah scroll, give it to the grandmother, who will pass it on to . . ."

Many people think they can play around with the Jewish religion and introduce some innovations for the good of the religion. A certain non-Orthodox leader wrote recently that he doesn't know what all those innovations have accomplished. He sees that the more innovations there are, the more estranged people are becoming.

But in those days, Germany and France exploded. Suddenly, instead of being third, fourth, and fifth-class citizens, they were *first-class* citizens and started looking up to and rubbing shoulders with the non-Jews. Many of them converted.

Others decided that they had to look like the non-Jews and not stand out so much. So instead of calling the house of prayer a *shul*, they called it a temple. Some of the *mitzvos* concerning relationships with non-Jews gave them problems, so they started doing some surgery.

Then they started with Bible criticism. The source of that was with German anti-Semites who wanted to destroy the authority of the "Old Testament." Bible criticism is still learned today, even among Jews, and it is a false thing for which they have no proofs.

They also obtained control over the Jewish communities, and they were the people who were recognized by the governments. Every Jew had to belong to the community, and they had the power to enforce decrees. They made it the ideal of the Jew to Germanize. There was nothing that couldn't be sacrificed. But in spite of all that, anti-Semitism surfaced and surprised them all.

Although there was anti-Semitism in Western Europe, at least the Jews did have some *official* recognition as equal people. In Czarist Russia, this was not the case. The majority of the Jewish people were in Russia. There were millions of Jews there. The only place where a Jew could be recognized as a human being was among the revolutionaries, in the underground. Their Jewish brains were really appreciated there. Without them, you would not have had Communist Russia. The Czar used to send them to Siberia, and some of them got out of there and went to America. These were the ones who established the labor movement in America and the labor movement in *Eretz Yisrael*. The strongest Jewish schools when I arrived in America in 1938 were the Workman's Circle labor schools. They had a tremendously strong system, with a network of schools all over the United States. Jewish history, for them, started with certain Yiddish writers, some of whom were very anti-religious.

THE MELTING POT

The American melting pot was a big mistake. When people live together, it does not mean that they have to erase their identities. I am what I am and you are what you are, and we respect each other. But I do not have to erase myself. We have to live together and respect each other, but we don't have to melt. Each nation has a contribution to make.

The idea of the melting pot was a reaction, and reactions are often extreme. When America started, there was great inequality in many countries of the world, and people came to America as a reaction to that inequality. The response to inequality — equality for all people — went so far as to erase individual traits. Again, this is what happened at the time of the French Revolution when the Jew became equal, and he ran so fast to meet the non-Jew that he thought he had to erase something in order to come closer to him.

◄§ But the Jewish people are not a people like other people. Our history does not move according to the same principles as the history of the rest of society. We are different, and whenever we try to assimilate, it does not work.

The legacy of the melting pot has been passed down to us today. There are those who would like to make only "100% Americans." They don't know the real value of being a Jew, so they're not willing to pay the price, which leads to the desire to be like the nations of the world. All too often, there is an inferiority complex among Jews.

It does not have to be that way. Every day we make a blessing in which we thank the Almighty that we were not made a *nochri* — a stranger — one who is not a Jew. The Talmud says there is a storehouse of souls, and from there each soul comes to a particular set of parents. I could have been born to someone else. But I know the value of being a Jew, and I am grateful to the Almighty for the fact that my parents are Jewish.

In the times of the *Beis Hamikdash* only a *kohen* could eat *terumah* (sacred food). It was forbidden to strangers. When I, who am not a *kohen*, want to eat *terumah*, I am considered a stranger. In the Chumash, our nation is called "kingdom of *kohanim*." This means that what the *kohen* is to the Jew, the Jew is to the rest of the world. If a person makes the blessing with that awareness, he does not have an inferiority complex. Nor does he have a superiority complex, any more than a *kohen* has towards the rest of the Jews. He simply has a different task.

◄§ As much as I like and respect people, there *are* some people today for whom I have no respect, not because I feel I am inherently superior to them, but because when it comes to morality they have placed themselves in the basement. There was a time when I knew that by not adjusting myself to anything which was not highly moral, I was respected by people. I am not sure that is the case anymore. I *am* certain that I do not have to be accepted by a society which is simply losing direction and destroying itself.

During the forty years that I was in America, I had the opportunity to observe Jewish education closely. But except for the *yeshivos* and some of the day schools, there are very few positive results of that education. The American youngster is a candidate for intermarriage. He has no real Jewish background. There is no reason why he should not fall for intermarriage.

◆§ There is a story of two farmers who go to buy potatoes for seed.

One comes in and sees on the counter the most beautiful potato. It's perfect, and he buys it. He doesn't realize that it is the newest invention: a synthetic potato, which looks and tastes great but which cannot reproduce itself.

The second farmer comes in and the beautiful potato is not there, so what can he do? He buys the broken potato, covered with earth.

The next year, who has the big crop? The one who bought the broken potato. The other one has nothing.

This has happened all over America in the field of Jewish education. Until the day-school movement started, there were only afternoon schools and Sunday schools. It was like people cooking with empty pots. They cooked and cooked, and nothing was produced. The youth in America were as ignorant when they came out of school as when they entered. There was no inspiration and no attachment to true Jewishness. They were planting fields of synthetic potatoes which produced nothing.

◆§ There was a student in my *yeshiva* whose father wrote me a
    classic letter. He said, "I want you to send my boy Herbie home! What's the idea?! He doesn't want to eat from my plates. He eats tuna fish from a can. I bought him a bike. I paid eighty-three dollars for that bike, and he comes home for the weekend and it's Shabbos, and he cannot use the bike. You better unkosher him and send him home, or I'll see my lawyer!"

When graduation time came, his father was at the graduation, and I asked Herbie what had happened to his father. He said, "Since my sister ran away with a non-Jewish sailor, he changed his mind."

The boy came to me and asked me to please do something for his sister. I arranged for her to go to a school in New York, and she went, but it didn't work out. She had never been exposed to any Jewish values.

She was a normal Jewish child. In that community at that time, any Jewish child who would not intermarry would be the exception. What background do they have? What motivation do they have not to mix, not to intermarry? If someone meets a non-Jewish person whom he likes, why not? It's normal, because they have nothing.

I once went into a photo store to take my picture for a passport. The photographer's wife came out and asked me if I was a rabbi. I said, "Yes."

She said, "Please, can you help me? My daughter is fourteen years old, and she was invited by her friends to join them in church for Easter. What can I tell my kid?"

This is the tragedy of Jewish children in the melting pot. You have to find some explanation to tell them why not to go to church. It means the child does not know anything positive about being a Jew. The child has no idea of 1,800 years of Church persecution of the Jews. He knows nothing. The synthetic potatoes did not produce anything. The field is dry, and vicious animals, such as a certain group of Jews who try to take Jews away from Judaism, can come and trample over it. Where there is Jewish information and Torah, they cannot touch anything.

A father told me that he was troubled by the fact that his son's school constantly had gatherings before the holidays, and they were indoctrinating the children with Christianity. So I said, "Take your child and put him in a Jewish school." He said, "Oh, no. That is impossible." He is a physician and a very intelligent man. But he knows nothing about *Yiddishkeit*, and he doesn't know what he has lost. He doesn't know what he is giving away. We hope that a miracle will happen with his child, as it is happening with so many Jewish children today. But without it, his family is a family of vanishing Jews, a dry field.

I have no problem with the children in a day school or in the *yeshivos*. They are the ones who will survive. This is what Moshe Rabbeinu says in the Chumash: "You who cling to Hashem will survive."

This also has a precedent in the Chumash. The Moabites and the Midianites called Bilam to curse the Jews, and he did not succeed. Then Bilam gave the king of Moab the advice to demoralize them by sending a host of girls into the camp. Twenty-four thousand people died as a result of this.

Those people wanted to mix with the girls, so they came out with a predecessor of the melting-pot theory. They said that the Jewish people have a function to be a light to the nations. "How will we inspire and influence nations if we keep away from them? We have to mix."

Afterwards, Moshe Rabbeinu told the rest of the people, "Look at what happened. The Torah told them not to mix. They thought they were smarter and were going to preserve the function of the Jewish people. No trace remained of them. You, who followed the Torah exactly as you were taught, are surviving."

SOLUTIONS

It is written that all the Jewish people are guarantors for each other, are responsible for each other. Because of this, I should feel that if there is anything I can do to save a Jew, to prevent him from falling away from Torah, I should do it.

The real source of the problem of assimilation is anemia. However, if someone is anemic and then contracts some contagious disease, it's too late to cure his anemia. You have to cure the disease. But concerning the others, who are merely anemic, you work on *that*. The anemia is caused by the lack of knowledge and positive experiences with Torah-true Judaism. The disease is the assimilation that results. There are many organizations today which are trying to work on the problem of assimilation. They have contact with assimilated Jews and try to pull them out. Others work with the anemic ones, the ones who are not yet assimilated but who are candidates for assimilation. The key in both areas is education.

Rav Saadia Gaon, one of our great philosophers and scholars, coined the phrase "We are a nation only by strength of our Torah." Torah means study, knowledge, and research. It also means that we place ourselves under the light and guidance of the One Who created us. The guard for everything is the study of Torah.

Professor Chavkin was a great man living at the beginning of this century. He was a Russian Jew who discovered an anti-cholera serum, and he went to India and saved many lives. Even today in India there are Chavkin hospitals, named after him. He became a *baal teshuvah* and left his entire fortune as an endowment fund for the support of *yeshivos* in Lithuania and Hungary. At that time it was very unusual to have endowment funds for *yeshivos*. It was under the management of the *Yiddishe Hilfsverein* in Berlin and continued until 1939.

He wrote a letter to a friend of his in which he told his story. He had been a child in a completely assimilated family in Russia. He wanted to learn medicine, but under the Czar it was impossible for a Jew to be accepted in medical school, so he went to Switzerland. He remained there for some time after graduation and became famous as a researcher.

He then returned to Russia, and the Russian government wanted him to accept a professorship in the University of Odessa. But a Jew could not take the position. So they told him that if he wanted to accept the job, he would have to convert to Greek Orthodoxy. He said in the letter, "I never knew anything about being a Jew, and I never gave it any thought. But now I said to myself, 'When it is suggested to me to give it away, let me find out what it is that I'm going to give away!' " Then he began to study and became a *baal teshuvah*.

The philosopher Franz Rosenzweig wrote about how affected he was by the Yom Kippur service. But he didn't learn Torah. He did not find the source of learning. He lived his Jewishness by emotion and by figuring out and doing things himself. If we could figure out *Yiddishkeit* by ourselves, we wouldn't have needed the revelation at Mount Sinai. Franz Rosenzweig had an emotional experience, but that's not a substitute.

Today, there are documents which show that millions of dollars have been pledged by the Church for the purpose of converting Jews. They use that money to train their people, to send them all over the world, to print material and mail it everywhere, to open cafeterias and orphanages and so on.

We, in combating the massive propaganda, are like the little David against Goliath. But we have a great strength: the truth. We have the job of building up our background of Torah-true education, knowledge, and experience. The more of a background we have, the more influence we will have. The more that we expose people to Torah, the more inspired they will become to live as Jews. If it's Torah, it's inspiring.

The key is education.

Yaakov Avinu had a dream. He saw a ladder going from earth to heaven, and angels were going up and down on it. If somebody would ask me to evaluate those angels, I would not evaluate them by which step they are standing on; I would evaluate them by which way they are facing. Is he facing up, or is he facing down? If one is standing on a high step but he's facing down, I know that he's going down. But if one is on the first step and he's facing up, I know that he's going up.

There were Jews in the past who had a strong Jewish identity and Torah knowledge, but they were not able to set up adequate educational systems, and generations were lost as a result. Today we see many people who may not be presently standing on a high step, but they are going *up*.

TORAH: OUR SURVIVAL

There was a very great yeshiva in the time of Avraham Avinu. This was the yeshiva of Shem and Ever, sons of Noach who lived very long lives. We don't know much about it, but we know it must have been very great because we know at least one of the students who learned there: Yaakov Avinu learned there for fourteen years, and when he started there he was not a youngster anymore. He was sixty-three years old. By that time he must have been very great, yet he went to their yeshiva to learn more. Why don't we have any traces of that yeshiva? We still have traces of the schools of Rabbeinu HaKadosh and others.

In contrast, Avraham Avinu was promised that his children would always survive. In the beginning of *parashas Lech Lecha*, Hashem says to him, "I will make you a great nation and I will bless you. I will give you a great name and you will be a blessing."

Nothing is timeless. Individuals have their young years, middle age, and then get older and disappear. It is the same thing with groups and nations. Nothing has indefinite survival. Why was Avraham Avinu promised survival?

An explanation may be that Shem and Ever had a great yeshiva, but they didn't canvass. They didn't go out and make the Torah available to others. That was for Avraham Avinu to do. He wasn't content just to satisfy his own personal needs, but went out of his way to teach others.

The Rambam makes it very clear in the first chapter of *Hilchos Avodah Zarah* (Laws of Idolatry) that this was the merit that gave Avraham Avinu timelessness.

There is a *midrash* that talks about another period and says that Avraham Avinu was rescued through the merit of Yaakov. Why did he need the merit of Yaakov? Why did his survival come through Yaakov?

An answer is that the blessing of survival could have been fulfilled in one of two ways: either by persecution, when we would not be permitted to assimilate, or through our bond with Torah, when we would not *want* to assimilate. Therefore, at the time when Avraham was promised survival, it could have been in a pleasant way or an unpleasant way. Yaakov — who represents Torah — made it the pleasant way.

Torah gives us survival, and in the most pleasant way.

Tragedy in Europe
and Rebuilding

It is the obligation of our lives to rebuild. We should know that in the rebuilding we are partners with Hashem Himself.

BAD LUCK OR DIVINE PLAN?

I am not sure that the name "holocaust" is correct. In Hebrew, it is called "*shoah*," which means "disaster." The word "aster" means "star," as in "asterisk," which is the symbol used to make a star. People have associated *mazal* with stars. A disaster means a bad *mazal*, something that just happens. *Shoah* then becomes something that is unexplainable. It is a tragedy that just happened, and we do not know why.

But there is nothing in Jewish life that just happens. Whatever happens in Jewish life is planned by Hashem. The Ramban says in his commentary on the Torah portion *Bo* that a person does not have a share in the Torah unless he believes firmly that whatever happens to a Jewish person, or to the Jewish people, is planned by Providence and is not a result of natural events.

If the words "holocaust" and "*shoah*" lead one to believe that these events just "happened" to us, then they are not the right words. Perhaps the word "tragedy" may be less misleading.

This did not just *happen* to us. It was not just bad *mazal*, bad luck. It was something planned, and it came from Hashem. The question is *why?*

The word *eichah* — "how" — is the most important question, and it is one that *we* cannot answer. It is a question that a wise man cannot understand nor a prophet explain. There are questions that human wisdom is capable of answering. There may be questions which are beyond human capacity to answer, but a prophet can answer them. Concerning the loss of the Temple and the destruction throughout history of so many millions of Jews, there is no wise man who can understand it, and even the prophet cannot answer. Only Hashem can give us the answer. "My ways are not your ways. My thinking is not your thinking," Hashem says. The answer has to do with the function of the Jewish people and the function of each and every Jew. In the Torah portion of *Haazinu*, Hashem tells Moshe Rabbeinu that the people will go through many kinds of experiences, and many of them will be very unpleasant experiences, and they will wonder why these things are happening. Hashem commands Moshe to tell the people the song of *Haazinu:* "Tell them that the song will explain everything to them. It will tell them what is going to happen and why it is going to happen." It is a very short and concise song, but it has inexhaustible information in it. In that song there is a prophecy for everything that is going to happen to the Jewish people.

Hashem says to Moshe Rabbeinu that the song is an *eid. Eid* in Hebrew has two meanings. One meaning is "witness," something which testifies. The other meaning is "warning." The song of *Haazinu* is both. It is a warning because it explains what the results of certain behavior will be. It is also a witness because we can observe throughout history that what has been predicted has come true. The Ramban writes that it is so accurate that even if we would find it written somewhere other than in the Torah, we would have to believe every word of it.

There is one statement there that says, "The tooth of cattle I will incite against them, with a venom of sand-crawling things." The *Sifri* says that there will come a time when peaceful cattle will become very destructive and full of venom.

   ∾§ The German nation was a militant nation for many generations, from the time of Bismarck. They had an ambition to conquer the world. But aside from this, the German people were highly intelligent and cultured. The Jewish people found assimilation easy and "grazed together in the same fields" with them. However, the Germans did not have quality of character. Suddenly they turned into such cruel beasts. There's no way to describe them. "Peaceful cattle will become venomous."

In 1937, an article which my father *zt"l* wrote appeared in *HaPardes*, a rabbinical magazine published in America. In that article he quoted a sentence from the portion of *Haazinu*. Moshe Rabbeinu says to the people, "I know that soon after my passing you will stray. If you leave the ways which I commanded you to follow, the bad results of your behavior will meet up with you at the end of days." The period in which they turned away after Moshe Rabbeinu's passing was the time of the Judges. It says in *Tanach* that there was idolatry among the Jews at that time.

My father wrote in that article, when Hitler was already in power and the clouds were very dark, that what was happening at that time was what Moshe Rabbeinu had foretold: The bad actions of the earlier generations of our nation will meet up with the nation at the end of days.

Thus, something was planned. There is a story which illustrates how something can be transported across three or four thousand years of history.

> A friend of mine in Detroit was a businessman. He was an expert in metal, and after the war he purchased a lot of broken tanks from military surplus. He knew that in the tanks were precious bolts. He extracted the bolts and made millions of dollars. The people in Washington didn't like this. They felt he had done something sneaky, and they stopped deliveries. He went to court and sued President Truman, as the representative of the government. The lawyer for the government claimed that it was not obligated to honor the contract because the man who signed the contract on behalf of the government was no longer in office.
>
> So my friend told his lawyer that he wanted to answer. He pulled a dollar bill out of his pocket and

went over to the judge. He said, "Your honor, the government is circulating illegal money. Look who signed this bill. That secretary who signed the dollar bill is no longer in office." He won his case.

The point is that a corporation, a people, a nation, survive the individual. A city can sell bonds and then three generations later the people will have to pay taxes in order to cover the costs, even though they were not the ones who borrowed the money. This is called a legal identity. The legal unit survives the individuals. It is the same with the Jewish people. We have our national identity. As a people we have a long life. We may invest in one generation and get our fortune five generations later. The Jewish people are a corporation.

We also suffer from collective sins. The individual's time for *teshuvah* is Rosh Hashanah and Yom Kippur. The nation's time may be different.

❧ There are some other tragedies that have national mistakes at their root. It says in the Chumash that when the spies came back from spying out the land and they gave a bad report, the people cried. Rashi says that this established a night for tragedy, a night for crying. Many tragedies later happened on this date, the ninth of the month of Av. That was the date of the destruction of the First and Second Temples. The Jews were exiled from Spain in 1492 on this day. The First World War broke out on this day in 1914.

INDIVIDUAL AND NATIONAL SUFFERING

In *Megillas Esther*, Esther speaks to the king about the tragedy that will happen to her nation and her people if they are attacked.

She is talking of "nation" and "people." These are two different things. The destruction of the Temple is a national tragedy. It reduced the Jewish people to a lower level. The Jewish people *with* the Temple and *without* the Temple are on two different levels. With the destruction of the Temple, our very nature changed as we became a people of exile. This happened two thousand years ago, and is happening today, because we still do not have the Temple. Thus, nationally, our loss is the same as the generation which was alive at that time. The tragedy did not become stale.

In terms of the tragedy in our generation, it was a national tragedy that so many millions were taken away from the Jewish people. The great treasures of the Jewish people were destroyed. But the Jewish nation is being rebuilt little by little. Perhaps we have not yet reached the level of Torah as it was before the war. We don't have the generation of the Chafetz Chaim and Reb Chaim Ozer and all the *gedolim*. But we know they are growing, and we'll have them, G-d willing.

But in addition to this national tragedy, the *individual* people who were present when the Temple was destroyed suffered terribly. There was horrible killing and starvation. In our time, there was the tragedy of six million individuals who perished. It is a tragedy of one and two and three and four and five . . . this individual, this individual, this individual . . . a multitude of six million individuals, not one total of six million. This was the tragedy which Esther was referring to in the second part of her question to the king: "How will I be able to witness the trouble which is going to happen to each one of my brothers and sisters?"

⊷§ In our time, to understand what happened to individuals and to come to conclusions for our own lives is almost impossible. It is not within human grasp to understand the compensation for the individual suffering. Most certainly there *is* compensation, but we cannot grasp it. We can only hold on to the Torah, and the Torah will lead us to some answers. Alone we are lost. Alone we cannot understand and we cannot rebuild, and it is the obligation of our lives to rebuild.

DAYS OF MOURNING, DAYS OF REMEMBERING

In order to perform the rebuilding, we have been given the capacity of "forgetting" to the extent necessary for us to do what must be done. Otherwise, if we were walking around carrying all the pain, the wounded hearts and the extraordinary memories, we would not be able to exist or to rebuild.

The Jewish calendar has seasons for everything. Rosh Hashanah and Yom Kippur are a time of self-correction. Succos is a special time for rejoicing. Pesach is a season for refreshing in our minds the basics of Jewish history.

The Torah wants us to be happy and rejoice, and for most of the year we continue with the rebuilding, but the Torah does not want us to be selfish. It wants us to have times to feel grief. If a person suffered, we should feel it, and it should be on our minds. Thus, the calendar provides for a three-week period preceding the ninth of Av in which we are restricted in certain areas of enjoyment in order to focus on the tragedies. The ninth of Av itself is a day devoted to remembering.

The Torah does not want us to suppress our feelings. In the week of mourning — *shivah* — for a departed relative, the first three days are considered in *halachah* as days for crying, and the other four days are for going over the memories of the departed. Nothing should be suppressed. The feelings should come out. All this reawakens our sensitivities, which prevent us from becoming too "forgetful," which would be a kind of cruelty.

◄§ This period of mourning during the three weeks, which is called *aveilus*, is a concentration on the national tragedy. We think of the losses to our nation resulting from the destruction of the Temple. We mourn for all that which we do not have any more. That *aveilus* can be awakened by concentrating on what happened to individual Jews. We participate in their sorrows and suffering. We picture what they went through while they were alive. This is compassion, where somebody else's grief is my grief. The opposite of compassion is cruelty, and refusing to mourn is cruelty.

Rabbi Shimon Shkop *zt"l* told me that in the 1920's he was in London and went to comfort a mourner who was sitting *shivah*. While he was there, someone borrowed a pen from him. At that time a fountain pen was a very expensive item. The person who borrowed it forgot to give it back to him. He could have asked him to return it, but he felt that it would be an offense to the mourners that somebody was sitting there and thinking of his pen while their minds were busy with their tragedy. So he didn't ask for it back and he lost a pen.

It shows that mourning — *aveilus* — involves concentration and brings one to great sensitivity. When somebody is a mourner, it takes over his mind. It doesn't leave place for anything else.

We have plenty of *aveilus*, whether it's for the Temple or for the events of our whole history. During most of the year we should be in a good mood, but the period preceding the ninth of Av is a period when we should control our mood in order to attain that sensitivity. It is part of our responsibility as a member of the Jewish "corporation," the Jewish nation.

◈ That is the emotional part of it. The Torah wants us to be sensitive to our tragedies and gives us a season for it. In addition to this, there is the intellectual part of it. These are the conclusions we draw and the lessons we learn.

PATTERNS OBSERVED

While comprehending what happened on the individual level is almost impossible, we have to understand, nationally, the hand of Providence which led it all to happen. As the Ramban says, we must believe that it was all for a purpose.

The lessons we learn teach us the nature of being a Jew and the nature of the Jewish people. Certainly there are no definitive answers to the questions involved, but we see that there are certain patterns in Jewish history.

There is one pattern recurring in our history, which consists of a period of affliction which is then followed by a period of reinforcement and strengthening.

This began in the earliest days: Yaakov Avinu had to run away from his brother, who wanted to kill him. He had to leave his home and the environment of his parents Isaac and Rebecca. He came to the house of Laban, who was a thief and a swindler. Before he arrived there, he went to learn in the yeshiva of Shem and Eber for fourteen years. This gave him additional strength to face the challenges of the environment of Laban. He sat in the yeshiva all that time, and like a camel which fills itself with a lot of water before going into the desert, he developed immunity to the surroundings of Laban. Living with a thief is not only a problem of "he will outsmart me." It is also a problem because if I have to interact with him constantly, I could very well lose my own honesty.

Jacob arrived at Laban's house as a single man. He was a refugee, his brother wanted to kill him, and he was exposed to the mercy of a thief. Twenty years later, he left there as a wealthy man with a family, and the Jewish family was already established. That was the first Jewish exile, and the house of Laban was the incubator.

Later Jacob and his children moved to Egypt as a family of seventy people. After 210 years of terrible oppression, they left as a large nation.

Later in history, the same thing happened. After the Babylonian exile, we came out much stronger as a nation than when we went in. The return from Babylon at the time of Ezra was a revival of the Jewish people whose effects are still with us today.

Even at the time of the second destruction, Rabban Yochanan ben Zakkai established his yeshiva in Yavneh, and this guaranteed the survival of the Jewish people. This pattern repeats itself in history over and over again.

I remember Poland. It's difficult to describe how the Jew in Poland was treated between the two wars. It's enough to say that there was a time when the newly married young couples in Warsaw had the furniture they purchased attached to the walls. The tax collector was not supposed to break walls, but aside from that, he would take away beds, dining room furniture, and everything else, so they built all the furniture into the walls. I remember in Baranovich when the tax collector came to a poor grocery man and took the scale away. He couldn't afford to replace it and had to close his business.

At that time America was a blessed land, materially, for the Jews. But where was the Jewishness? Where was the vibrant Jewish life? In Warsaw. In Vilna. Not in New York or Monsey. If there is today a Jewish revival in America, it was brought about, to a great extent, from the remnants that thrived in Europe during the period between the two wars. There was a genuine blossoming of great men during those difficult years. It's very difficult to accurately describe the greatness that existed in those days in that part of the world. And this all occurred amidst twenty-one years of affliction.

In these days, after the terrible tragedy of the Second World War, we see the blooming and flourishing Torah communities in *Eretz Yisrael* and the rest of the world. All that we see today was unimaginable before the last war.

WHERE WAS THE BOSS?

In his booklet Ikvesa d'Meshicha (The Footsteps of the Mashiach), my father zt"l talks of the days preceding the arrival of the Mashiach. He quotes the statement of the Sages that in that period "the face of the generation will be like the face of a dog." He explains that when a man takes a cane and hits a dog, the dog bites the cane. He thinks that the cane hurt him. He doesn't realize that there is a man behind it who is holding it.

This was the mistake of the spies who were sent by Moshe Rabbeinu to spy out the land. They "bit the cane" and established that night for crying. This is often our mistake. The correction for it is more education in order to understand that Jewish history is led by Hashem.

On close scrutiny, it seems that all anti-Semitism has a function, and something good results for us. Our survival is not always ensured in the most pleasant way, through our adherence to Torah. There seems also to be a pattern of assimilation and non-adherence to Torah throughout our history which precedes the periods of affliction, resulting in our strengthening and continuing as a nation. When it seems that we are in danger of disintegration and we have run *en masse* to the non-Jews, that's when the non-Jews push us back, for our own survival.

When Yaakov Avinu went down to Egypt, he was afraid. So the Almighty said, "Do not fear. I shall go down with you, and I shall surely bring you up." *Sforno* says that Yaakov Avinu was told, "You have to become a distinct nation, and while you are in Canaan you will never form your identity. Go to Egypt, where Egyptian law says that the Egyptians cannot sit at the same table with the Hebrews. They will keep you in a ghetto, and you will become a people."

§ A man is sick and has to have an oxygen tent. If somebody comes in and finds that man in bed, he might say, "That man is strange. He lives in a tent." But he is making a mistake. The oxygen tent is only to carry him through a crisis, and then he'll live like a normal person. The oxygen tent that we have is anti-Semitism. It has a function, but it is only to get us over a crisis, until we can get ourselves together and "breathe" and live without it.

Yaakov Avinu says to his son Reuven, "You are hasty like water. You cannot have leadership over your brothers. You cannot be a leader because you are hasty, quick to change."

A solid keeps its own shape. A liquid will not keep a shape unless you put it in something. It has to have some outside limitations to keep its shape. People who can control themselves are symbolized as a solid which can keep itself together. People who follow their temptations are "hasty like water."

Similar to that is the nature of a nation. A person — or a nation — has to have either an inside force keeping him together, or if not, there have to be outside pressures.

When Jacob and his family were to be in Egypt, Hashem was telling him that they did not have anything to keep them together. They had not yet been given the Torah. They had to go through the pressure-cooker experience of Egypt in order to become a nation. Jacob and his sons, who were destined to become a great nation, had to go through that in order to be molded into a people capable of receiving the Torah.

In fact, we find that three days after crossing the Red Sea, the Jewish people began to fall apart. The reason was that they had not yet been given Torah; without the external binder, Pharaoh, we need the internal binder, Torah.

§ When we received the Torah, we were warned against assimilation, which means giving up our identity. The prophets also warned us. Ezekiel said, " 'When you will say that you will be a nation like any other nation,' says the Almighty, 'it will never happen. I will come to you with great anger.' "

This means that we are to be an eternal people. It is not a guarantee for the individual, but it is a guarantee for the nation that this people will continue its identity.

We may not fully understand the reasons for the patterns, but we know, as intelligent people, that there is a limit to what we can understand. Only unintelligent people think they have to understand everything. We were told by the Almighty and by his prophets to hold onto the Torah and our identity, and we can observe the patterns in history that result from our adherence and non-adherence. It is a matter of certain natural reactions which are built into nature. This is not the same as *punishment*. Punishment is something which overrides the natural order of things. If something comes about as a direct result of behavior, it is simply called *natural*.

From the day that the Jewish people were prepared to be formed, we had that kind of a harness. Ideally, Torah is what should keep us together. If not Torah, G-d forbid, then we need a container. Somebody has to press us together. That is the function of the enemy. That is why Esau was born as a twin to Jacob. That is his function. Anti-Semitism is a kind of preservative, albeit not a pleasant one, which keeps us from assimilating.

The Almighty turned the hearts of the Egyptians to hate His people. This was the blessing which did not let them assimilate, and which gave them the ability to develop as a people and to be ready to receive the Torah. In fact, it is taught that one of the meanings of the name *Sinai* is the idea that together with the Torah which was given there came down a *sinah* — a hatred — for the Jews.

ـ§ In reality, the anti-Semites are not fighting the Jews. They are fighting the Master of the World. Persecuting the Jewish people is as far as they can reach in fighting Hashem. They do not want His presence to exist in the world, and when His presence came down with the Torah which was given to the Jewish people, that hatred became directed against the Jews. In Egypt, Joseph placed the Jewish people in their own land — a ghetto. There, they lived with the presence of Hashem in their midst, even before the Torah was given to them, and the Egyptians were not bothered by it. When "the land became filled with them," when they broke out of the ghetto, then the anti-Semitism started.

The Rambam, in one of his letters, comments on the verse "Do not be like a mule who does not understand and has to be harnessed by reins." He says, very simply, that an animal has the ability to move but does not have the understanding to control his movements. He has a natural instinct to avoid areas that are dangerous for him. But he does not know not to hurt someone else or not to destroy things. Therefore, we have to harness him. He is a hazard. "You are a human being. You have intelligence, and you have a conscience, and a feeling of what is right and wrong. Do not be like an animal. Then there will not be a need to harness you, to control you with reins."

THE SPIRIT OF THE NATION

Rabbi Chanina ben Teradyon was one of the ten martyrs who suffered a cruel death at the hands of the Romans. They tied him up and wrapped him with the *sefer Torah* (Torah scroll) and set it on fire. His disciples were standing there and asked him, "Rebbe, what's happening now?" He said, "I see parchment being burned and letters flying up in the air." This means that the tortures are on the body, but the spirit of the nation has never been touched by the tortures. The spirit of the nation may have become weakened by times of luxury and convenience, but not by tortures.

In the Book of *Devarim*, Moshe Rabbeinu was preparing a new generation, most of whom had not been at Sinai, to enter the land. He left them a testament, which he gave over at the end of his life. He repeated many of the Torah's teachings, including the Ten Commandments. At the end, in the portion of *Ki Savo*, the Jewish people entered a covenant. There were many blessings and curses given, and they were warned that if they would not act properly in the land, their blessings would turn into curses.

After this, the portion of *Nitzavim* starts with "You are standing today before Hashem." Rashi says that when the people heard all those curses, they said, "Moshe, we are going to be broken and crushed." He answered, "Do not be afraid. Your sufferings will make you stronger. They will be the cause of your survival." From this we can learn that perhaps we are surviving not *in spite* of suffering, but *because* of suffering.

The Jew has a function. In spite of all the inconvenience of being a Jew, I still open the *siddur* in the morning and I say, "I thank You, Hashem, for having picked us out from all other nations." The tragedy of the secular Jew is that he feels that he has been picked out to be hated and persecuted. It's a pity.

I have one important thing in common with the secular Jew. The anti-Semites hate us both equally. But the secular Jew is paying a price, and he doesn't know what he's getting for it. I pay the price, but I know what I'm getting for it, and it's worth it. There are certain values which I can attain by being a Jew. But if I don't like those values and I am made to pay a price, then I'm like someone who pays for something and doesn't receive the merchandise. Then I am unhappy with paying, and I feel like a fool.

In fact, when Hitler came, the people who were the first to commit suicide or lose their minds were the assimilated Jews. They believed they were Germans and did not understand what was happening. The religious Jew knew that he was paying a price, but he received something for it. He considered himself blessed that he had the opportunity to be close to the meaning of being a Jew.

When I come off an airplane, for example, and I am hungry, I pay a price for being a Jew. If I wouldn't observe Jewish law, I would stop in any coffee shop and get a bite to eat. Instead, I go hungry for a while. I gladly do it.

But a person who has never been exposed to Jewish values finds the price too heavy and tries to minimize it. He thinks that by catering to foreign values he will minimize his liability.

In the *shtetl* (small town of Eastern Europe) the Jews had many great men, intellectually and ethically. To a great degree, the heights that were reached then have been destroyed, although they are being rebuilt. A well-known writer said about the Rogatchover, one of the great Talmudic scholars of the last generation, "Give me one Rogatchover and I'll cut ten Einsteins out of that one man." When intellectual and ethical values like that are something we aspire to, then we look to our own people for them. But when material values are what we aspire to, then the non-Jew next door has better values than we, and our ambition is to be like him.

There is a book called *Meshech Chochmah*, by Rabbi Meir Simcha of Dvinsk. He was one of the great *geonim* (Torah geniuses) of the Chafetz Chaim's generation. He passed away in the 1920's, so his book must have been written around the time of the First World War or before. He writes, on the Torah portion *Bechukosai*, that after the Torah enumerates the curses which will descend upon the Jewish people if they do not keep the Torah, it says, "When they are in the land of their enemies, I do not despise them. I do not reject them and do not break My covenant with them, because I am Hashem their G-d."

Reb Meir Simcha says this means that when the Jews will settle in a land and think that this is their home, and they will think that Berlin can take the place of Jerusalem, the Master of the World will not let them get lost in that land. He specifically refers to Berlin and says that there will come a storm that will tear them out from their roots there. If Berlin becomes their Jerusalem, there will come forth destruction from Berlin like the destruction of Jerusalem.

The Torah says, "I will not forget them and will not break My covenant with them, while they are in the land of their enemies." How will the Master of the World do it? By bringing about a holocaust, says Reb Meir Simcha.

Everything in Jewish history is planned, and it leads up to something. The Jewish people are compared to sand on the seashore. This is because when one digs a hole in the sand on the seashore, in a short time it fills up. Likewise, no matter how big a hole our enemies will dig into the Jewish people, eventually it will fill up. But Hashem needs us as partners to build up the nation.

After the mourning of the ninth of Av, we read on each of the next seven *Shabbosos* a *haftarah* of consolation. Each one tells us that Hashem will console us. Immediately after the mourning, the Torah wants to build us up again. We have to live, we have to create. We have to *do*, and we have to build. The seven *haftaros* of consolation tell us that what has happened is not destruction. It is plowing. It's all plowing and sowing for the great plant of Mashiach.

HOLOCAUST MEMORIAL DAY?

We have nineteen *berachos* (blessings) in the *Shemoneh Esrei* (main prayer of the liturgy). Eighteen were established by the Men of the Great Assembly. The nineteenth was composed during the first century, around the time of the destruction of the Second Temple.

There was a need to make a special prayer against troublemakers and informers. Rabban Gamliel was at the head of the nation, and he decided that we had to add one prayer against those who were making problems for us. He made an announcement: "Is there a man who can compose a prayer to put in the *Shemoneh Esrei?*" After searching, they found one man by the name of Shmuel HaKatan, and he composed it.

But some of the greatest men in our history were in that *beis midrash*. Rabbi Akiva was there, as were Rabbi Tarfon and Rabbi Elazar ben Azariah. Why did Rabban Gamliel have to look around for a man to compose a prayer?

The Rambam wrote a letter which is called the *Letter to the Yemenites.* Among other subjects, he talks about comparative religions, and he says about certain religions that "what they are trying to do is to copy the real knowledge — the genuine law. And all they succeed in doing is like a sculptor who makes a statue of a human being, and there is no life and no *neshamah* there."

Then the Rambam, as a physician, goes on to describe the muscles, the blood vessels, the nerves — the components of the human body. The sculpture doesn't have any of that, he says. It's just an appearance of the human face and body, and that's all.

The Rambam is saying that the *Toras Chaim* — the living Torah — has real *life* in it. When I look at my finger, I see simply the finger. But that finger, in order to remain alive, has blood vessels, nerves, muscles — many systems that support it. But when *I* look, I see a finger.

Torah is the same. In Torah, the appearance is not as important as what is inside. And *inside* there is a great deal.

Shemoneh Esrei is the same. The *Tur Shulchan Aruch* counts how many words there are in the *Shemoneh Esrei*, and there is a meaning to that count. He also counts how many letters there are for the same reason. On the surface it looks innocent and simple, but it is very skillfully composed in order to appear that way.

A word of Torah is loaded with energy and tremendous power. You cannot just make a prayer. If it is to be made the Torah way, it has to contain all the *life* of the Torah. Rabban Gamliel was looking for somebody who had that skill.

The same concept is behind the idea of making a national memorial day and national day of mourning. We cannot make copies. The Chazon Ish was asked about that, and he said that we don't have people who are great enough. We cannot just create *times*, on our own initiative. We don't have the people to create them. We have no Shmuel HaKatan in our generation. Communities may have their own local commemorations, but we do not have commemorations on a national scale. If we have to re-experience some things of the Holocaust, we put it into our experience of the ninth of Av, because we have that day already. That day commemorates the event which was the source of all our exiles, and includes within it all our exiles.

> *Hashem said when He took us out of Egypt, "I saw how they tortured him. I heard him crying. But his real pain nobody knows. I know his pain." If someone is in pain, no one else really knows how deep his pain is. The Almighty says, "I know his pain."*

Tangible and Non-tangible Worlds

The non-physical is the life and sustenance of everything physical.

THE NON-PHYSICAL WORLD

The *gemara* says that every blade of grass has an angel which beats it and says, "Grow." The meaning of the *gemara* is that there is a non-physical source behind everything that we see. Today's science is coming very close to this understanding by speaking of matter as energy. It is in the right direction.

When the Torah talks about the non-physical world, it says, ". . . and Moshe went up to Hashem." It sounds as if Hashem is in the attic, and Moshe has to go up to him. But the word "up" does not refer to a physical location at all. We say *Der Eibishter*, "The One Above," and it is just a figure of speech, because it has nothing to do with space. Hashem is everywhere, not just "up." "Up" means out of the physical and into the non-physical area. It means right here too.

There is another word which we also use to refer to the non-physical world. When we refer to *Shamayim* — Heaven — we mean the *non-physical* source of everything which the Master of the World has created. When we talk of the creations in *Shamayim*, such as *malachim, seraphim,* and *ophanim* (various types of angels), we are also talking of non-physical creations. When we, who are physical beings, talk about these creations, it is similar to talking about the ocean to a person who has never seen marine life. Someone tells him that in the ocean there are all kinds of creatures. He will have one name for them all — fish — because all he knows is that there is a certain element — the ocean — that he has not looked into, and that certain creatures exist in that element. He makes no distinction between one creature and another.

Similarly, all we know is that there is a great ocean of a non-physical world, and that non-physical world is also filled with beings, but we don't know what they are. The people who wrote about them — the prophets and the mystics — understood these forces.

THE HUMAN BEING AND THE NON-TANGIBLE

The human being is a combination of both the physical and the non-physical. The body is physical, but the soul — the real *life* — is not.

The Rambam says that the actual reality is the non-tangible, not the tangible. A human being's true life is non-tangible. His clothes are tangible, as is his nose and his whole face. But our essence is the personality, which is non-tangible. We talk to each other, but we do not talk *to* a face. We talk *through* a face. We see our bodies, but we don't see each other.

In everything, the essence is the non-tangible. Everything tangible leads to a non-tangible. With a human being, the tangible is the body; but it has no value unless there is life inside it. So the value of the human being is not in the tangible, but in the non-tangible.

There are countless levels of non-tangible, and in order for us to handle them, they have to be dressed up in something tangible; and that tangible is the description we use to describe them. Without that, we cannot imagine them.

Likewise in a human being, in order for us to relate to each other, each one of us is dressed up in a body. In order for the soul to be in our world, it has to be dressed up in a body.

~§ Torah is also like this. In order for us to handle Torah, it has to be dressed up in a tangible garment. That dressing took forty days. Those were the forty days that Moshe Rabbeinu spent on the mountain, receiving the Torah. It took that long for it to come to a level where we could deal with it. When we learn Chumash, we touch the letters, but there is *life* inside the letters. According to the Rambam, the Torah is a replica of the entire universe. But it is not visible in the letters that we see. It is what is *in* the letters.

> There is a story about Rabbi Yochanan who was walking with his *talmid*, Rabbi Chiya bar Abba. As they passed a certain house, Rabbi Yochanan said, "That house used to be mine, and I sold it so that I could support myself and have time for learning." Then they passed by a vineyard, and he said, "That vineyard was mine, and I sold it for the same reason."
>
> Rabbi Chiya bar Abba started to cry. He said, "Rebbe, what security have you left for your old age?"
>
> Rabbi Yochanan answered, "Don't you realize what I did? I gave away something which took only six days to create, and I received in return something which took forty days to give."

The world was created in six days, and Rabbi Yochanan gave away worldly possessions: things which were created in only six days. In return, he received Torah, which is so deep that it took forty days to give — forty days to clothe so that we could handle it at our level.

THE HUMAN BEING AND THE WISH OF THE CREATOR

Whenever we go deeper, we come to something which is more intangible than the previous level. What makes things exist? What keeps them existing? Only the wish of the Creator. This is the most non-tangible.

The human face has many variations. A photographer knows that he can pick up several variations of the same face. An artist also knows it. We say that if not for the wish of the Creator, these expressions would not exist. Even for one human face, there are many wishes of Hashem that it should exist. There is one wish — one *will* — for there to be an ear on a human being, and another one for a nose. Everything that exists is an expression of the wish of Hashem. If not, it wouldn't be. *There is no other force but the wish of the Creator.* We don't understand the essence of this wish, but this is a fact.

◦§ There is no end to all the expressions of the wishes of Hashem. It is taught that the world was created with *lashon hakodesh* (the holy tongue) — a composition of letters. If you take anything and you go to its root, you find the will of Hashem as an expression of letters. If you would trace electricity to its ultimate source, for example, you would find a combination of letters which express this kind of energy. Therefore, if you take every detail of the entire Creation, it is the *will of Hashem* as expressed in a combination of letters. The Ramban says that all of the Torah consists of the Names of Hashem. A *name* enables us to identify something. From the Torah we learn the expressions of Hashem — His Names. If you trace everything to its roots, you come to these combinations of letters — these Names. We think we trace it as far as the atom, but it goes much deeper.

The entire Torah consists of Names of Hashem. This means that the entire universe is in Chumash. The Ramban says that because of this, if a single letter is missing from a *sefer Torah*, the entire *sefer Torah* is invalid. This is because it has come to represent an incomplete universe. The entire universe is represented in the *sefer Torah*, and if a letter is missing, it is a damaged universe.

We learn that "*Talmud Torah* — the study of Torah — has no limit." This means that the obligation of studying Torah — a replica of the unlimited universe — has no limit. The Master of the World desires that the soul of the human being should be like a mirror in which the entire Creation is reflected. In the study of Torah one can reach deeper than the tangible level to the non-tangible; through immersion in the unlimited Torah one can "peel off the body" and find the intangible life in it. When this level is reached, the soul begins to reflect the Creation. A wish can be a wish in one's heart, and it can also be an expressed wish, in words. The wish in one's heart is less tangible than the wish expressed. The limit that the human being can reach in understanding and experiencing the wish of Hashem is to come to the expression, but not to the heart. Those who understand more, understand deeper and deeper expressions. But we can understand only the *expressions*. The essence of the Almighty Himself is beyond our reach.

INTANGIBLE, TANGIBLE, AND LAW

In nature, only shapes change. Substance, or matter, does not change. If laws are tailored to the naked substance, the undressed matter, as are the laws of Torah, they will never change.

ᴥᴥ We have, from the Chumash, a classification of *mitzvos:* *mishpatim, eidos,* and *chukkim.*

ᴥᴥ The *mishpatim* — judgments — are things which are logical.

These are the social regulations in the Torah. We understand that there is a social need for these laws.

The *eidos* — testimonies — are actions which should keep us conscious of our obligations as Jews. Saying the *Shema* is one example. A person has to repeat to himself every day that Hashem is One. *Tefillin* are also a testimonial. They are a reminder that Hashem took us out of Egypt. Shabbos is a reminder of the Creation of the world, Pesach of the exodus from Egypt, and Shavuos of the giving of the Torah. The observances related to them are called *eidos.*

There is another group called *chukkim.* They are decrees or statutes. We do not know the reason for them. Rashi says a *chok* is something which cannot be explained. Furthermore, there is a direct relationship between something which is inexplicable and something which is unchangeable. Let us explain this.

Many years ago, a friend of mine read a medical article in the Jewish paper in Poland. It explained that eating milk and meat together is unhealthy. He came and told me how happy he was to hear that. I told him "It's no *mazal tov.*" As long as we don't know a reason for the Torah prohibition against eating milk and meat together, nobody is going to change it. But as soon as it is said that it is unhealthy, then in five years some medical genius will discover a remedy which will enable it to be eaten without danger. I would be able to take his medicine and eat milk and meat together. Therefore, as soon as you explain it, you shorten its life span. But if it's inexplicable, it's unchangeable.

This is a practical answer, but the truth is even deeper than this. Why are things inexplicable? If the Torah recommends or commands something, there must ultimately be a good reason for it.

The answer concerns the limitation of our ability to understand the intangible. There is no human conception of matter without form. One thinks of a piece of paper and right away he has an image of it. That form is changeable. The same matter that is in gas could be converted into liquid or into a solid. Therefore, everything that is humanly conceivable is expected to change because conditions will inevitably change. However, the essence of the thing is durable. It will never change. That essence is intangible and inexplicable.

There are two verbs in Hebrew related to the act of writing. *Koseiv* means to write; *chakok* means to engrave. You write on the surface, but you engrave *into the material*, beneath the surface. That is what *chok* is. It is a law engraved below the surface, tailored to the pure substance, and thus the real reason for it is beyond the limitation of our abilities of conception. This is why we call it "inexplicable."

Human laws are not durable because they are tailored to the conditions of existence, to non-durable conditions. These are changeable forms. Social regulations, for example, are made to fill a certain need in a certain situation. If you are living in an apartment house, at a certain time of night you cannot play your musical instrument because you will wake up your neighbors. That rule is made to order for the condition of living in that apartment house and having neighbors. Rules are always made to fit conditions.

Conditions change. That is why rules have to change and why we constantly have to make corrections in the civil code. However, it is only the form that changes and not the essence. Therefore, since we cannot understand anything of pure essence, we cannot conceive of any regulation which is not changeable.

Essence itself is not changeable. Laws that are tailored to essence are not changeable. The Torah is tailored not to the outward form, but to the essential, ungraspable matter. It is on this that it is said, "The wisdom is hidden from the sight of every living being." The wisdom is the essence of the *mitzvah*.

Even the *eidos*, which have a religious explanation, and the *mishpatim*, which have a social explanation, are all based ultimately on *chukkim*. In the *Haggadah*, the wise son asks the father, "What is the meaning of all the *eidos*, the *mishpatim*, and the *chukkim*?" The father answers about the exodus from Egypt. Then he says, "He told us all the things which were good for us. Then He gave us all the *chukkim*." He ignores the *eidos* and the *mishpatim*. He considers that everything — all 613 *mitzvos* — are in fact *chukkim* at root.

The *Sefer HaChinuch*, which gives roots and explanations for the *mitzvos*, warns us that the explanations which we can understand are not the only ones. The reason for this is that if the *mishpatim* or *eidos* would have their root in tangible reasons, they would not last. They last because they are tailored to the level of essence. There are some things about them we can understand, but the real reasons for the *mitzvos* are beyond our ability to understand. Every *mitzvah* has a number of results, but we should not mistake the results for the essence of the *mitzvah* itself. The real source of the *mitzvos* is "hidden from the sight of every living being."

TANGIBLE, INTANGIBLE, AND ETHICS

Everything which Hashem has created in the world has many kinds of purposes. The real function of food is to supply energy to the body and to replace vitamins and minerals. We could take food intravenously and also receive what we need. Why do we have to chew it and taste it — good taste, bad taste, salty, sour, sweet?

There are a number of functions involved in taste. Taste warns you when the food is spoiled, and taste helps digestion. The *nachash* (serpent) was punished by having to eat dust. He eats because he has to eat, but he doesn't enjoy his food. All living creatures enjoy their food, except the *nachash*.

So the fact that we enjoy our food while we feed our bodies necessary nutrients is a gift that Hashem gave us. But the enjoyment is a product, not a *reason*. As soon as a person starts eating for enjoyment only, he may make himself very sick — the product has become the *goal*.

There are also products of *mitzvos*. These are what the *Sefer HaChinuch* gives as some reasons and effects of the *mitzvos*. This is difficult for the non-Torah world to understand. The non-Torah world thinks, for example, that the laws of social behavior are made in order to keep society functioning. The Torah says it is not like this. They are *chukkim*, just like all the other *mitzvos*. But when you observe them, the *result* is that society behaves and functions properly.

This erroneous conception which is held by so much of society has contributed to so many of the problems and the crime that we have today. People believe that ethics are for our convenience. So now we have a new approach: ethics of convenience. Thus, whatever is convenient for me are my ethics. Whatever is convenient for him are his ethics. This leads to a situation in which there is no order. The words "law and order" will have no meaning, and abuses will abound.

But the real ethics are a *chok*. This is how Hashem created the world. When you follow the real ethics, you have your product, and your product is happiness, convenience, and comfort. This means also, that unless you follow the commandment "You shall love the Lord your G-d" — the intangible — you cannot properly fulfill the commandment "Love your neighbor as yourself." One who attempts it without the awareness that it is ultimately a *chok* will find that his conception of "Love your neighbor" will constantly change and fluctuate, according to social conditions, and will eventually lead to disorder.

THE CHALLENGE OF THE INTANGIBLE

The *mitzvah* of the "red heifer" is given in the Torah, and it says there, "*Zos chukkas haTorah* (This is a *chok* of the Torah)." It is here that Rashi explains that a *chok* cannot be explained.

> There is a famous *midrash* about a non-Jew who comes to Rabban Yochanan ben Zakkai and says, "You Jews are superstitious. When a person touches a

dead body, you say he is impure. Then you take a red heifer and you burn it, and you take a little of the ashes, mix it with water, sprinkle it on the person, and now you say he is pure. It's all superstition; how could it have any effect?"

At that time, the non-Jews had a certain type of sickness that they believed was some kind of an evil spirit. Rabban Yochanan ben Zakkai asked him, "What do you do when someone has the evil spirit?" The non-Jew answered: "We take some grass, put it on fire, and when the evil spirit smells the smoke, he's afraid of that smoke and goes away."

Rabban Yochanan answered, "It's the same with the spirit of a dead man which passed to the one who touched him. It's like that evil spirit, and when it senses the ashes with the water, it departs."

The non-Jew was happy. He had an answer. But the *talmidim* of Rabban Yochanan ben Zakkai said, "You pushed him away with a straw (with something which is nothing, an answer which will bend and break as soon as you touch it). How would you answer us? How, in fact, does it work?"

He answered them, "It is not the dead who makes impure. It is not the water which makes pure. We do it because Hashem has instructed us thus. We do not know what it is. Hashem gave us a law and said, 'It is not within your capability to understand.' "

Rabban Yochanan ben Zakkai told the non-Jew that the red heifer worked exactly like their spirit. But if somebody had asked him, "Do you understand how the grass works with the evil spirit?" would he have said that he understood? He didn't understand. So why did the non-Jew accept the answer?

He accepted it because to satisfy the mind doesn't always require understanding. Habit also satisfies the mind. If you see a thing constantly being repeated, you don't question it. You take it for granted.

⋘ At an eclipse of the sun, a lot of people try to understand what is going on. Very few ask how it is that the sun is shining the rest of the time. This is no less of a question than the other. But if you see it daily, you take it for granted and you don't question it.

Rabban Yochanan ben Zakkai sized up his questioner and realized that he wasn't a deep intellectual, and that it would be enough if he gave him an answer that fell in line with his habitual thinking. "You take for granted what happens with your spirit; you'll be satisfied with a simple answer for the red heifer also."

But his *talmidim* were sharper. They said, "What kind of an answer is that?"

He could have given the non-Jew the answer that he gave to his *talmidim*. But the non-Jew would have said, "Nothing is beyond me! I don't understand this, so I don't accept it."

This leads to an interesting observation: It is the small mind, the unintelligent person, who thinks he has to understand everything. If he doesn't know something, it doesn't exist.

If one says, "Truth is what I experience or what I reason," he is not correct, because there may be things that he doesn't experience and which he cannot reach with reason, due to the normal limitations of the mind.

⋙ The *talmid chacham*, the sharp intellectual, realizes that there are many things he doesn't understand, and he accepts that. He is able to say, "Fine. There are things that I don't understand."

There are many people who think they are smarter than the Torah. They say, "Why do we need this? What I don't understand is wrong." It is impossible to discuss it with them.

Thus, we learn from the *parshah* (portion) of the red heifer about the limitations of human understanding and about the intelligent person who is not afraid of a challenge to his understanding.

TRUSTING THE INTANGIBLE

We need to know that we are not *chachamim*, and that we need to trust Hashem.

The Chafetz Chaim used to tell a story about the king whose friend tells him that he is going to a social gathering. The king says to him, "Enjoy yourself, but promise me one thing, that you will not take any bets."

The next day the man comes in and the king says, "How was it?"

"Wonderful."

The king asks him, "Did you take a bet?"

The friend answers, "Yes."

"But I told you not to take one!"

"Your majesty, it was such a stupid thing they bet with me. It was a sure win. They took a bet with me for fifty thousand rubles that I have a wart on my back. I rolled up my shirt, proved that my back is clear, and collected fifty thousand rubles!"

The king answers, "You fool. They took a bet with me for a hundred thousand rubles that they could make you roll up your shirt in public!"

The Chafetz Chaim used to say, "Let not a person think that he is smarter than the Torah. You never know what's behind it."

Kabbalah:
Questions and Secrets

If the Creator is so friendly to us (and we find that the Creation is friendly — we ruin it, but it is friendly), why are we born with the torture of having questions for which we have no answers?

Kabbalah contains the answers to those seemingly unanswerable questions.

There are no secrets in Torah — the question is only concerning which level you have reached.

The word *Kabbalah* means *received transmission* or *received tradition*. It is one part of the Oral Torah which was not written down explicitly. It was written down in very difficult codes, which compels a student to turn to someone to help him decipher them. Thus, to learn Kabbalah we have to depend on a person-to-person transmission.

The question remains even after the basic definition: What is Kabbalah?

KABBALAH AND PHILOSOPHY

The Rambam says that Kabbalah is "the subject which philosophers have pondered for generations." One description of philosophy is to say that philosophy deals with questions which are very clear, but the answers to these questions are not so clear. It's not science. In science, you can have a question, then you make a discovery, and you have an answer. But there are other questions which we cannot answer precisely.

What is the human being? All we see of the human being is his body. We see his limbs. The body is a garment, and the limbs are tools that the human being utilizes. But what is the human being, the person himself? The question is very clear. But for the answer, you can only speculate. This is the area of philosophy. It deals with those questions for which we cannot find a clear answer.

There is no doubt that there is such a thing as moral law, but what is it? Why should we follow it? What is the definition of good and bad? These questions are as old as humanity itself. No clear solution to moral problems has yet been found by the human mind. Morality is still a subject of philosophy and is taught as such in the universities. If even a relatively definite solution of the moral problem would have been found, morality would have been transferred from the philosophy department to the field of science.

We see that the Creator is good to us. He wants us to enjoy ourselves. There is a special *berachah* which we make when we go out in the spring and see a plant blooming. It's a joy to see. We make a *berachah*, and we thank Hashem that He has created things just for our pleasure. So why did He give us such an area that brings us to sadness and torture? To have a question and not find an answer is a torture.

The Book of *Koheles* asks the same question. It is essentially a manual of philosophy. King Solomon, the author, quotes many philosophical theories. He discusses many issues. In the end he says that no theory answers the questions. He says, "After you have heard everything and you see that nothing answers you, be in awe of Hashem, observe His *mitzvos*, and you will have your answers."

He is saying that there are answers given to us, even if we cannot yet understand them, and that they are in the Torah.

INFORMATION AND GATES OF UNDERSTANDING

The answer to all the philosophical questions was given to Moshe Rabbeinu to give over to the people. This is what Kabbalah is: the answers to all the unanswerable questions. The questions may only be unanswerable to us on our level. The answers are not "secrets," and they are not "mysteries." They simply exist on a higher intellectual level, which we have to be intellectually prepared to reach.

The Rambam explains that *gemara* is a mind-grinding tool. The entire function of it is to grind, to sharpen, and to develop the mind to be so refined that we will be able to understand the questions and the answers. While we are learning, our intelligence is being shaped, refined, and trained in handling abstractions. It is being led towards the abstract parts of Torah. He says in the *Introduction to the Mishnayos* that the purpose of all learning of Torah is to prepare the intelligence to be able to come close to *hasagas haBorei* (understanding the Creator). Some things are hidden because we are not prepared. They are too fine to be handled with the normal tools of our unprepared intelligence.

It says in the Torah, "Let My lessons pour on you like rain, My sayings like dew; like storms on grass and like drops of liquid." The *Sforno* likens this to the different ways in which people learn new information. For those who are great, there is so much information that it pours on them like rain. The average person also receives information, but it is less in quantity, relative to his capacity, and it is pleasant, like dew.

The great man may find information as he is learning that will shock him, shake him. That is like storms on grass. The grass represents the green cover of the earth. The great people see the entire picture, as in one sweep of green grass covering the earth. They are constantly making discoveries which they did not expect and are constantly being shaken up by them.

When we learn Torah, we must know that Torah is a replica of the universe, and its depth is endless. The *Mishnah* in *Pirkei Avos* speaks of this and says that "it is not up to you to finish the work." Imagine, for example, a large park with a gate at the entrance. Once you go through the gate, you can go as far as your feet can take you. There is no end. But you go as far as you can.

This is what a "gate of understanding" is. It is an opening, and each and every one can go in. One gate leads to another, and it is endless. They are all different sections of Creation. The levels are infinite, and each person grasps on his own level. All that Hashem wants from us is to *go*, to proceed as far as we can.

INTELLECTUAL LEVELS AND SECRETS OF TORAH

We have to understand what is meant by the expression "secrets of Torah." It is not proven that we cannot have answers to our questions. One thing *is* proven: The unaided human mind cannot find an answer to many problems and questions of philosophy. The great philosophers have tried for thousands of years, and no one has come up with answers. They have come up with theories, but not clear-cut, definite answers. Thus, by experience, we have to conclude that the human mind cannot find an answer to those questions. But it is not proven that the human mind cannot grasp an answer if it is given. However, that answer has to be given *from without*, from a higher source. The assumption is that logically, once an answer is given, it can be grasped. If it cannot be grasped, it would be a terribly illogical arrangement. It would mean that I can be tortured with questions for which I cannot get an answer. It would not be fair to be given questions such as these. And we find that the Creator *is* fair.

We say that those answers were given together with the revelation of Torah. However, not everyone is ready to grasp the answer when it is given to him. Would you teach mathematics in pre-kindergarten? You don't want to keep it a secret from the children. But they are not ready for it.

Every person has two levels of intelligence. There are things he can find out and solve on his own, and there are things which he cannot find out on his own; but if someone comes and gives him the answer, he will understand it.

All the areas where a person can find out things himself may be called level A. The level where he can understand the answer, if given to him, may be called level B. Not everybody has the same level of intelligence.

Reuven has a certain level where he can answer questions himself. This is A. But the next level for him is B. Here he cannot answer, but if you will explain it to him, he will grasp it.

Shimon is a little more intelligent. What is B to Reuven is A to Shimon. But what is B to Shimon is entirely off limits to Reuven — he will not understand it even if someone tries to explain it to him.

The highest person has an A which may be understandable to the person just under him, if explained, but the highest person's B is off limits to everyone else.

Therefore, when we say there are questions which the human mind cannot answer, we are talking about questions which a very few can understand when they are given the explanations.

There always remains something that is beyond B to everyone. That may be the actual *essence* of the Almighty Himself, which Moshe Rabbeinu asked to have revealed to him, and which he was told was impossible even for him. He was told by Hashem, "Nobody can see Me and live."

But the answers to all the other questions were given to Moshe Rabbeinu, and passed on to us. The higher levels are called the "hidden" parts of Torah. But there is no mystery. They are just something of a higher intellectual level that one has to be prepared for by going through the "brain-grinding" and refining process of learning and observing Torah. They are understood in their fullest and deepest meanings by only the highest level people. Each person is obligated to proceed as far as he can go, even though "It is not up to you to finish the work."

TRANSMISSION AND THE CONVEYER BELT

It is important to understand the mechanism with which we explain things to each other. What we are doing at those times is transferring ideas from mind to mind. A conveyer belt is needed to accomplish this. That conveyer belt is *language*. If a person never saw a table in his life, I might want to give him an idea of what a table is. First, I myself have to understand that the table is a complex of elements. Does the other person know elements? Does he know shapes? Shape is also an element of a table. Does he know color? Can he figure out how to put things together? Then I tell him, "Listen, this is of a hard material. The shape is like a rectangular board. But I want the board to be at the level where it is easy for me to use, so I take something and I support it. Then I raise it, and I have it at the level where I can do something with it."

This is the process of translating ideas. You take apart the concept that you have to explain and bring it down to its elements. You give him the elements and you also tell him how to construct it. There-fore, if I explain something to you, there are preconditions that you, as a *listener*, must possess. You have to be familiar with all the elements that I am discussing, and you have to be able to follow instructions in order to construct something from what I tell you. If my listener is missing one element, he will get a picture, but not a true picture of the table. If he has all the elements but he cannot follow instructions on how to construct it, then he will have the legs of the table on top of it.

Therefore, every teacher must be very careful that the students get the right ideas. Otherwise, the teacher may say something and the student will understand something else. Every teacher has had that experience.

Hashem wants us to be knowledgeable people. Therefore, He gave us the Torah, which is a replica of the universe. Along with that, we were given the *mitzvah* of *talmud Torah* — learning Torah. We find that by learning Torah, we learn about the entire universe.

Hashem wants us to have that information, but He wants us to have the real picture. Therefore, the Torah warns us not to teach people who are not prepared for that teaching, because if they are not prepared, they will learn something other than what you tell them. The Rambam makes a statement in *Hilchos talmud Torah* (The Laws of Torah Study) that "if you have a student who is not ripe to understand you, what you teach him is non-sense, because what *you say* makes sense, but what *he hears* is nonsense."

◦§ There is a story about two Sages in the *gemara*. Each was particularly expert in a different part of Kabbalah — one was a master of *maaseh merkavah* (the wisdom of the holy Chariot) and the other was a master of *maaseh Bereishis* (the Creation wisdom). They said, "Let us teach each other. You teach me your wisdom and I'll teach you mine."

The first one taught the other one *maaseh Bereishis*. Then he said, "Now it's your turn to teach me."

The other answered him by saying, "I cannot teach you. While you were teaching me, I saw your level, and you are not ready for it."

This means that what I can understand, I understand. What I cannot understand, I am better off not touching, because I will only *misunderstand* it. Misunderstanding is not just a zero. It is a minus.

When a teacher is teaching, he should always be checking to see if the student is on the level of the teaching. This limits misunderstanding of the things that the Torah wants us to know.

There is no end to the depth of any created thing. It is only a question of how far you can go. If you take a match apart and you consider all the laws of physics in it, you can make a lifetime study out of one match.

Similarly, Torah has no end. But if you are not ready for it, you can burn yourself.

Kabbalah gives you what is beyond the normal limits in the search for truth. But man does not always search for truth. He often looks for convenience. Some people think that Kabbalah is some kind of a "power" which they can call upon and use. This is often how people look at Jewish mysticism. Their entire concept of mysticism centers around the performance of miracles. They think Kabbalah contains blessings or gimmicks. *That kind of mysticism is close to paganism.*

Certain academics — known as "experts" on Kabbalah — talk about Kabbalah, but they do not know what they are talking about. They have their own imagination of something, and they are teaching it as "truth."

Often they think of Jewish Kabbalists as people who found "the key" — a good thing — and these Kabbalists keep it for themselves, not giving it to anyone else.

There *are* some things that are forbidden to be taught to three students at a time. But the "experts" misunderstand the reason for it. The reason is as follows: If one of the students misses a word, he may ask another one, "What did the *rebbe* say?" In the meantime, while those two are conversing, the *rebbe* is continuing with his teaching because there is a third person to listen. Then the first two will miss something. However, if just two people are being taught, it is impossible that the *rebbe* will continue teaching. If they are talking with each other, he will stop.

It is forbidden to learn *maaseh Bereishis* even with two students. If one teaches two students, he adjusts the teaching to an average between the two. Therefore, neither one can get the maximum. And maaseh Bereishis needs so much precision that you cannot trust your explanation unless it is directed to just one student.

Maaseh merkavah is so deep that it is not trusted to be handed over to even one person. It is forbidden to teach it to even a single person, unless he is a chacham (wise) and understands himself; then the rebbe may guide him to discover more for himself. Chacham refers to one who knows the whole Torah, in quantity. This means that he has learned and understands the entire Mishnayos, which is a compressed miniature of the whole Torah. This is quantity, but not depth, because in depth there is no end.

THE HIDDEN ART OF TORAH

> We live in a period of great scientific discovery. Many people are finding out about the wonders of Creation. But instead of coming to be in awe of the Creator, they go in the opposite direction. Therefore, to learn the marvels of Creation, it is safer for us to learn it in a tosafos — in a page of gemara. There we also see the wondrous beauty of the Creation — in a depth without end.

There is a concept of mechuseh, something which is covered up, and nistar, something which is completely hidden. If I put an object in my coat, with the bulge visible, that's called mechuseh. You do not see what I carry, but you see that I carry something. The Books of the Prophets are in the category of mechuseh. Sometimes there are very difficult sections there that absolutely require investigation and interpretation in order to be understood on any level. One knows there is something being said other than the simple, surface meaning. That's not nistar.

In Chumash, which is in the category of nistar, the art is so great that you don't even notice that there is something under the surface. Rashi, in his commentary on Chumash, points out for us the places where we need to investigate further. He has put together in Chumash all the elements which he felt a Jewish person needs. But there are difficult parts in Rashi also, which bear further investiga-tion ... In the beginning of Bereishis it says, "Let there be a firmament in the middle of the waters." Rashi says that the firmament is exactly in the center between the lower waters and the upper waters. The Ramban says that what Rashi is saying here is one of the most hidden statements of the Torah; he says, "Do not expect me to explain it, because even those who know should not explain it; and even more so, myself."

Now why did Rashi write this if it is so deep that it cannot be understood?

Let us give an analogy to explain this. Torah is compared to bread. The *Midrash* says that Moshe Rabbeinu did not eat bread or drink water for forty days. The *Midrash* then asks, "What did he live on?"

And the answer is, "On Torah. From the light of the *Shechinah*, (the Divine Presence)," and then it says that the angels also exist on the light of the *Shechinah*.

Moshe Rabbeinu, during the time he was being given Torah, received his sustenance from Torah, which is the bread of the *neshamah* and the food of the personality.

When you eat bread, the first thing you do is chew it. When you chew it, you enjoy it. We say that Hashem is *tov u'meitiv* — He is good and He gives goodness. This means: *He is good* — He gives us food; and *He gives goodness* — He enables us to enjoy it. But this enjoyment is not the function of the bread. The function is nourishment, and it is not nourishing until it is swallowed.

It is the same with Torah. When I am learning, that which I understand is like the taste which brings me a feeling of great satisfaction and enjoyment. But there is more: When the bread — the Torah — goes into the system, it *nourishes*; it goes in with an entire depth, the entire power and strength of Torah, much more than I consciously know, just like food which is digested automatically and nourishes the body even though I am unaware of it.

There are times when a person needs a food, but it is too hard to chew. So it is put in a pill, like vitamins. It is swallowed, and then one has the needed element without having to taste or chew it.

When Rashi put together all the elements we need in learning Torah, there were parts which he knew we could not understand. When the Ramban talks about that part in *Bereishis* which we cannot understand, he is saying, "It's a vitamin pill. Swallow it. You need it, and you'll get what you need. But don't try to understand it — you'll break your teeth!"

Whether we realize it or not, Torah is full of tremendous force and brings great inspiration.

ON THE ENERGY OF TORAH

A simple battery is full of energy. An atomic bomb looks very innocent. But with one press on an innocent-looking button we can release enormous energy. Likewise, the whole of Creation looks very innocent.

One of the greatest miracles of Creation is not the energy, but the *locking in* of that energy. Kabbalah refers to the *locking in of energy* as *tzimtzum*, and shows that this is *gevurah* (power, strength). The *tzimtzum* of Creation is the greatest power that exists.

The world was created in such a manner that the raw energy was *locked in* and chained down to us on our level, in order for us to be able to approach it.

The Torah is also a creation by the same Creator. Torah is also full of tremendous force — dynamite. Rashi says in the beginning of the Book of *Bereishis*, that the original light of Creation was much more powerful than the light we have for our use, the light of the sun. The Creator said, continues Rashi, that the original light was too good to give into the hands of the wicked, so He hid it away and reserved it for the righteous in the World-to-Come. *It was hidden in the Torah.*

When we learn Torah — when we swallow it — we don't realize the fullness of its inspiration and its power. It is full of tremendous power and energy.

A Vision For the Future: Mashiach

In Israel there are two lakes, the Yam Hamelach (Dead Sea) and the Kinneret. The Kinneret is full of life, and the Yam Hamelach has no life in it at all. It's interesting that the Kinneret — the life-giving lake — takes water in and gives water out. The Yam Hamelach only takes water.

When we speak of "the time of Mashiach," we are speaking of the time when the entire human race will come to its senses and become givers instead of takers.

HUMAN NATURE BEFORE MASHIACH

The human being is a social creature. A person was created to exist among other people, to be concerned for them, and to be a *giver*. When people are concerned for each other, it's a blessing which gives them their happiness, and their pleasure and joy in life.

The Rambam talks about this in discussing the happiness of Yom Tov and Purim, and he understands that the greatest enjoyment comes from making someone else happy. Our enjoyment is not in what we get for ourselves, but the satisfaction that we receive when we do something for someone else. By being concerned with what I can contribute, I constantly have the satisfaction of having done something for someone, and this keeps me happy and also radiates happiness.

If you live in a society of *takers*, your existence is not pleasant and your life is not safe. The question of whether people are givers or takers is the difference between paradise and hell. In a relationship between husband and wife, for instance, there is always a give and take. Suppose you have two different households: In one household the husband and wife are interested only in what they can get from each other. Each one is concerned only with his own happiness. In the second household, each one is concerned with what he can do to make the other one happy. You don't have to think twice to know which home is paradise and which home is hell. In a natural home as defined by the Torah, there is a lot of happiness.

Love consists of giving, not taking. Rabbi Elya Lopian said that when a person says, "I love fish," he means he loves *himself*, not the fish; the fish must be sacrificed for him. This is not love. This is simply taking. When we love fish, we are takers, not givers.

When people are takers, it could be said that they are infants. When an infant is crying, you cannot go over and say, "Don't cry, you are disturbing somebody." An infant doesn't consider anything but himself. Maturity consists in realizing that we also have to be concerned about our surroundings.

In today's society, you find seventy-year-old infants. Imagine a world populated primarily by infants. How could you control social behavior and have peace and quiet?

The Torah clearly tells us that this kind of infantile behavior is incorrect and is the cause of much of the social unrest and disturbance that we see today. In fact, we have developed into a society in which *taking* is a natural thing. Everyone does what he wants, with the result that we have massive violence throughout society.

Once, in the "good old days," children made lemonade and sold it at a roadside stand. You paid your five cents and received a cup of lemonade. Today, social ethics could be likened to a barrel of lemonade prepared by the kids for sale the next day. During the night one kid drinks a cup and replaces it with a cup of water. "What harm can dilution by one cup make?" Each kid in turn does the same thing. In the morning, there is a barrel of water instead of a barrel of lemonade. Social ethics and conscience have followed the same path. Each one takes his glass of lemonade, with the result that nothing real is left.

The natural human conscience is supposed to be a guide to help us develop proper rules of behavior, and to help us create a society which will be positive. But it is difficult to talk about a human conscience today because it has become so corrupted that it has almost no similarity to a natural one. Our natural intuition of what is right and wrong has been so influenced by what other people think and by the values that are accepted that the light of our conscience is dim.

We have another guide, in addition to the conscience. That guide is Torah. The word "Torah" means *teaching*. Our Creator gave us His teaching. The human being, if he is searching for true values, is lost without Torah. The Torah is the service manual of the universe. When I buy a washing machine, I want to have a service manual. If I don't know how to operate it correctly, I may cause a short. I may tear up one of the parts inside. Every machine has a service manual.

The world also needs a service manual, in order that we use it properly and not tear it up. The Torah is that manual, and it says, "Don't do this! You'll cause a short! You'll destroy something! Do *that*, and it will run smoothly!"

THE END: SELF-DESTRUCTION OR MASHIACH?

There was once a society like ours. That was the society which perished in the Flood at the time of Noach. The Torah says that the earth was filled with robbery, with people grabbing from each other. That is the kind of generation which is self-destroying. Yet in the Chumash, Hashem has sworn that there will not be another flood on that scale. So what will He do when there is a society that is so similar to the pre-Flood society?

An answer lies in a statement of Rashi in the beginning of Chumash *Bereishis*. Rashi says there that the natural light which was created during the six days of Creation was much more powerful than the light we have now. The Creator saw that the light was too good to give into the hands of the wicked. It was hidden away and reserved for the righteous in the World to Come. We were given, for our use, a fraction of the light of Creation.

It is similar to a toy hammer given to a child. We would like him to get used to using a hammer or a screwdriver so he will learn to become handy. But we don't give him a real hammer. We give him a plastic one, because the fact that he is an infant may bring him to cause damage to himself or to others with a real hammer. In the meantime, he has something to play with, something to learn with, but it's a toy.

Likewise, we were given a fraction of the powerful light of Creation. What did we do with that fraction of the light? We created atomic energy, and we are very possibly about to destroy ourselves.

But since Hashem has sworn in the Chumash that we will not actually be destroyed, I have the feeling that He is watching us. Mankind can go up to the very border of self-destruction but cannot destroy itself completely. Now, since we cannot be destroyed completely, what is Hashem going to do when there is a society that is so similar to the pre-Flood society?

Instead of bringing a Flood, He is going to bring Mashiach. There are prophecies that state that at the time when society is on the very brink of destruction, it is precisely then that the Master of the World can bring His kingdom to manifest itself in the world. Many of the things prophesied about that period of time — for example, the *baal teshuvah* movement — are occurring now.

All this may not come about easily. It is written that there will be very great tribulations in the period preceding Mashiach. The students of Rabbi Elazar asked him, "What should a person do to survive the great tribulations preceding the time of Mashiach?"

He answered them, "He should busy himself with Torah and acts of kindness."

Acts of kindness bring rewards that are far greater than those which may be expected from the acts themselves. An example is a person who is standing in line to buy an airplane ticket, and he is short one dollar. He knows that the clerk cannot sell him the ticket without the dollar. So the man behind him sees his predicament and comes to his assistance with a dollar.

Later, that person who lent him the dollar is in a situation where he needs someone to put up a $5,000 bond for him. The first person hears about it and says, "He did me a favor once. Now, I'll do him a favor."

The act of *chesed* (kindness) performed by the man in the airport terminal brought him a reward far greater than that which he may have *earned* with his dollar. He may only have *earned* a dollar, but he *deserved* more.

This may be something like a remote-control garage door. A person pushes a button in his car and it opens the garage door. Things that are done *here* have a remote effect later, and in another place. *Chesed* — kindness — is one of those things which may have effects later. It is even possible that an act of kindness done by someone may have an effect on his great-grandchildren.

In this way, Rabbi Elazar meant that a person who occupies himself with acts of kindness during the time preceding Mashiach's arrival, when much of the world will be *taking* from each other, will receive a reward far greater than that which he earned: his kindness will stand out so much and be so meaningful that he will deserve to be saved from the tribulations which will engulf the world at that time.

MANKIND COMES TO ITS SENSES

Hashem created the human being as the pinnacle of Creation — the purpose of the entire Creation and the most important part of it. Instead of rising to the challenge and the task, man is destroying himself morally and endangering himself physically.

This is a serious question. It's not extraordinary when a human being opens a business and the business doesn't do well. It's normal that sometimes they succeed and sometimes they fail. But is it possible that the Creator, the Holy One, Blessed is He, opens a business and the business fails?

But the answer is as follows. In a business, if you want to know whether the business is failing or not, you have to have a bird's-eye view. Sometimes a business has different departments; for example, the advertising department may make signs and put them all over the highways, and a lot of money is being put out. Yet the business flourishes because there is a sales department which pulls in money and more than compensates for the money put out by the advertising department.

Likewise, when a person opens a business, at first he invests and invests and invests. Then, in a relatively short period of time, he can make enough sales to justify all the investments. All the investments are finally producing. But you cannot be sure of that until the end.

It is the same with a single human being. It says in *Ethics of the Fathers* that a person should repent one day before he dies. It means that even if a person's entire life was wrong but one day of his life ended up good, it has such a great value that it compensates for and salvages all the years of wrongdoing, all the years of "bad investments." One of the qualities of repentance is that it brings to correction the time which was spent in the wrong way of life.

If this is true for a single person, then it is true for the entire human society, all of mankind. After so many thousands of years of wrong behavior, if it will end up with correct behavior, it will be so valuable that the whole venture will not have been a failure.

The time when the whole human race will come to its senses is the time of Mashiach. Mashiach is the promise that the Master of the World will not let this world end as confused and chaotic as it is now.

The prophet Isaiah says that in the age of Mashiach people will beat their swords and make plowshares out of them. It shows how stupid we have been. The Master of the World gave us metals to make plowshares and feed the world. Instead, we made killing tools with those metals, and there are people who don't have enough to eat. So the prophet says that there will come a day when humanity will come back to its normal mind, and instead of using what was given to us for curses, we will use it for blessings. We were originally given those blessings, but we made curses out of them.

When Mashiach comes, we will start living a normal, natural life, as the Master of the World created us. Life will be pleasant — people will become givers and contributors instead of takers — and together with that will come all the blessings.

A VISION FOR THE FUTURE

My father *zt"l* used to say that the miracles occurring at the coming of Mashiach will be greater than those which occurred at the time when the Jewish people left Egypt. In everything that happens, there are two aspects: There is the part which we see, and there is the part which is behind it, which we cannot see. At the coming of Mashiach, the total of what we see, of what is *revealed*, will be greater than both the revealed *and* the hidden aspects of the events at the leaving of Egypt.

It is like saying that whatever we have experienced is like a bad dream. When a person is dreaming, anything is possible. When he wakes up — when he "comes to his senses" — he sees that it was only a dream, not reality.

When we wake up and Mashiach comes, we will realize that it was all just a bad dream. But it's very, very hard to understand. All the people who have been tortured, all the people who have been lost — how can we say it was a bad dream? How can we say such a thing? But it seems that all our worries will be over, like a man waking up and saying, "ay, it was just a dream."

But even knowing that intellectually, there is still something inside that cries out and says, "How can you say that it was simply a bad dream? All those people who suffered? For them it was not a dream. It was *real!*"

◦§ Many times a child asks me to help him cross the street. The child doesn't know how to cross the street, but he knows that if he is holding on to an adult, everything is okay. We should know that we are in the same position. We can only hold on to the Torah, and the Torah will lead. Alone, we are lost and without answers.

HEART OF STONE, HEART OF FLESH

There is something remarkable in the Book of the prophet Zechariah: "I will pour upon the house of David, and upon the inhabitants of Jerusalem, a spirit of grace and supplication; and they will look towards Me, regarding those whom the nations have killed. And they will mourn for the slain as one mourns for an only son and shall be in bitterness over him as for a firstborn. On that day there will be a great mourning in Jerusalem ... the entire country will mourn, and families will mourn."

What is remarkable is that the *gemara* says that all this will happen *after* Mashiach comes. *That's* when there will be a great mourning and people will be crying bitterly. We would expect the opposite: that after Mashiach comes, people should be rejoicing!

We should understand this as follows. We know that the Master of the World wants us to build. But how can we build in the face of such tragedies as we have experienced throughout our history, and especially in recent times? How can we have the heart to start all over again and rebuild?

Noach had the same question after the Flood which destroyed all of mankind. In the Chumash, it says that after the Flood, "Noach, the man of the soil, started out by planting a vineyard." Rashi says that the word *vayachel*, "he started," can also mean "he profaned himself." Rashi means to ask, "Why did Noach plant a vineyard?" He came right off the Ark, and the first thing he did was plant a vineyard.

But we can understand Noach. He came out of the Ark, and everything in the whole world was dead. We can imagine his feelings. He had to comfort himself, and he wanted wine for that. But Rashi means to say, "When you survive, there is no time to comfort yourself. It is time to start building. Plant wheat."

But our hearts are broken in the face of our tragedies!

The answer is found in the prophecy of Zechariah, who tells us that now is not the time for crying, as if to say, "*Later*, you will have time to cry." Ezekiel the prophet says that after Mashiach arrives, "I will remove the heart of stone from your flesh, and I will replace it with a heart of flesh."

This means that until Mashiach comes, we are walking around with a heart of stone, compared to that which we will have later. We are insensitive, *so that we can carry on.* If we truly felt the pain of what we have been through, we would be paralyzed with grief; so we are protected by our heart of stone. Ezekiel says that after Mashiach comes, and conditions will be such that we will be able to grasp what happened and still exist and be active, *then* Hashem will give us sensitivity. Suddenly we will remember what we kept in the back of our memories, and suddenly it will become a part of us. And *that's* when the crying will begin. At that time, there will be a "great mourning," as we remember what happened.

Until that time, we will be given a special gift: the capacity for forgetting. If a person would remember all the tragedies which he passed through all his life, it would confuse him. It is truly a gift that some things can be forgotten. It is necessary for our existence.

There are two aspects to all our suffering over the generations: the national disasters and the individual disasters. From the point of view of the national disaster, we will realize that all our suffering led up to something: to the time of Mashiach. We will *see* and understand how it all fits in. From that point of view, we will be able to say that it was all a bad dream and that the questions we had were not really questions. We'll see that it was only the limitation of our ability to understand that prevented us from understanding, but by the time the answer will be revealed to us, we will be able to bear the tragedy and the learning from it, because we will be able to understand it as a total picture.

The prophet Isaiah talks about this, and says that after Mashiach comes, we will say, "I thank You, G-d, for having been angry with me, because when Your anger will go away, I will be consoled"; that is, I will understand everything. Then all this will make sense to me. Then we will be able to afford to have a heart of flesh, and then we will be able to cry and to survive.

We will also cry for the massive *individual* suffering over the years, as we reawaken and experience again the pain of all those individuals. We will have a true heart of flesh. Before the time of Mashiach, the tragedy of the Holocaust, for example, is too immense for us to bear. It is not a tragedy of six million people. It is a tragedy of one and two and three and four and five ... this individual and this individual, and that individual ... a multitude of six million individuals. It is so immense that if we would dwell on this, we would not be able to exist.

THE SECOND CAMP

Another key to this idea is found in Chumash, where Jacob was on his way to *Eretz Yisrael* and he encountered his brother Esau and feared that Esau might destroy one of his two camps. He said, "If Esau will come to one camp and destroy it, let the remaining camp be the one which will save our future." The remaining camp would have the job of rebuilding what was destroyed. We ourselves see that many tragedies have happened to the Jewish people, but we are still surviving. *We* are the second camp.

We have to build homes, we have to build families, and we have to rebuild the great Torah institutions. With wounded and sensitive hearts, none of the great institutions of learning would have been rebuilt. We would collapse. We would lose our minds.

So Hashem gives us a heart of stone, so that while we feel *something*, we do not lose our minds. . . which, in reality, we *should* do! When Mashiach comes, it will be different.

There is a sentence in Chumash which refers to this idea. It says, "You will be blessed in the city and blessed in the field." The commentary *Baalei HaTosafos* in Chumash says, " 'You shall be blessed in the field' refers to Zion, as it says, 'Zion shall be plowed like a field.' "

What is the *blessing*, if Zion will be plowed like a field? Surely this is an expression of destruction? The answer is that plowing is not destruction. Plowing is a preparation for planting. But in the process of planting, plowing looks like a destruction. So the *Baalei HaTosafos* say that the blessing of Zion is that its plowing will be the foundation for planting.

Likewise, in the Book of Jeremiah, it says in the first chapter, "You have been appointed. . . to crush and destroy, to build and plant." It refers to a crushing which is in order to build, a destroying which is in order to plant.

The prophet Zechariah says that days of fasting will be turned into days of rejoicing. Why is it not enough to say that after Mashiach comes, we will not have to fast? Why will the fast days *themselves* become days of rejoicing? The prophet is hinting that all the tragedies were just plowing for planting. Then, when we find out what was really happening, when we understand the real meaning of those days, they will be days of rejoicing.

We don't understand it, and we can't understand it. There are many things that we can't understand.

On that day, when we will be able to thank Hashem for the tragedies, we will understand. But at the same time, the tragedy is a tragedy, and we will cry.

◆§ But there is a possible problem with an insensitive heart. A heart that is not fully sensitive could lead us to be insensitive in those places where we *should* be sensitive. It could lead to cruelty. The Jewish people are called *rachmanim*, people who have compassion. If we are given hearts of stone, then our characters could be destroyed. This is why the Jewish calendar has provided us with periods of mourning. It tells us to go on during the year and continue building. But there is a period during the year when we concentrate on the tragedies.

◦§ At the end of the Torah, in chapter 30 of the Book of *Devarim*, it says, "After all these things will happen to you, the blessing and the curse which I have given you, you will take it to your heart among all the nations where Hashem has dispersed you. And you will return to Hashem and you will listen to His words . . ."

We are not prophets: How do we listen to the words of Hashem? The answer is that when we learn Torah, we are listening to the words of Hashem. So it says that there will be a time when suddenly, after the tragedies, blessings and successes will happen. We will turn back to Hashem, with learning. "Then Hashem will bring your captives back to *Eretz Yisrael*."

We have a feeling that we are that generation which Hashem is bringing back to Himself. Eliyahu Hanavi (Elijah the prophet) says that He will bring back parents to their children. He will bring the Jewish people to the redemption.

It looks like this is beginning now. People from everywhere are returning. There will be hundreds more and thousands more, and it will grow faster and faster. These are the lucky ones, because they know where Hashem is leading them and they are in the advance guard that Eliyahu is leading.

These are the people whose connection with Torah is making them sensitive to the process of redemption. Recently I had to advise a young couple to leave *Eretz Yisrael* and go back to Canada because of *parnassah* problems — there they will be able to earn a living in such a way that they can dedicate much more time to Torah learning. Shortly after our conversation I received a telephone call from the young woman; she was anxious about the following question: "What will happen if Mashiach arrives while we are out of *Eretz Yisrael?*" She was thinking that perhaps they would be excluded from the whole process if they are not here. I answered as follows: "I am not sure whether Mashiach is going to be selective.

However, if he is, I feel that he will be selective not on the basis of where a person is, but rather on where a person belongs."

Mashiach's time will be a very happy period because people will live in a correct way. If the manual of Hashem's Creation is followed, there is happiness, there is pleasure, there is everything. So the happiness of the days of Mashiach will be the result. It is not the goal: the goal is the Honor of the Divine Presence. The goal is to do the will of Hashem, and the result will be a happy period.

❊　❊　❊

May all our prayers be favorably accepted, for each and every individual, and for the Jewish people as a whole.

✒ Glossary

Glossary

alav hashalom, aleha hashalom: may peace be upon him, her

apikorsus: heretical ideas

aveilus: mourning

Avraham Avinu: our father Abraham

baal teshuvah [pl. *baalei teshuvah*]: one who returns to Torah
observance

bachur [pl. *bachurim*]: yeshiva student

bar-mitzvah: age of majority for boys, 13 years

bas kol: a voice from Heaven

beis midrash: study hall of yeshiva

Beis Hamikdash: the Holy Temple

berachah: blessing

Bereishis: Genesis

bitachon: trust

bris: covenant; circumcision

chacham [pl. *chachamim*]: wise man, wise men

Chafetz Chaim: Rabbi Yisrael Meir Hacohen Kagan of Radin
(d. 1933)

cheder: Torah elementary school

chelek: portion

chesed: kindness

chok [pl. *chukkim*]: commandment, the reason for which entirely
transcends human understanding

cholent: dish of mixed ingredients which cooks overnight; served
on Sabbath

Chumash: the Five Books of Moses

daas: knowledge

daven: pray

Devarim: Deuteronomy
echad: one
emes: truth
emunah: faith
Eretz Yisrael: the land of Israel
gadol [pl. *gedolim*]: great man
gaon [pl. *geonim*]: Torah genius
galus: exile
gemara: Talmud, the Oral Law
geulah: redemption
haftarah [pl. *haftaros*]: selection from Prophets read on Sabbath
    after Torah reading
Haggadah: text of the Passover night service
HaKadosh Baruch Hu: the Holy One, Blessed is He
halachah: Torah law
hasagas haBorei: understanding the Creator
Hashem: lit. "the Name"; G-d
hashgachah: Providence
havdalah: ceremony marking transition from Sabbath to week-
    day
hesped: eulogy
Kabbalah: mystical teachings
kashrus, laws of; laws of permitted and forbidden foods
kedushah: holiness
kehillah [pl. *kehillos*]: community, communities
kibud av v'em: honoring father and mother
kohen [pl. *kohanim*]: priest
lashon hakodesh: the holy tongue
lashon hara: forbidden speech
lishmah: lit. "for its own sake", for the sake of Heaven
l'shem Shamayim: for the sake of Heaven
maaseh Bereishis: the Creation wisdom
maaseh merkavah: the wisdom of the holy Chariot
Magen David: star of David
Mashiach: Messiah
mechitzah [pl. *mechitzos*]: barrier
mechuseh: covered

Megillah: scroll; the Book of Esther

melachos: creative actions prohibited on Shabbos

mentsch: lit. "person", a decent and refined individual

mesechta: tractate (section of Talmud)

mezuzah: lit. "doorpost", parchment with specific Torah portion affixed to doorposts of Jewish dwellings

Midrash: Torah sources which delve deeper than the plain meaning of the Scriptural text

Minchah: afternoon service

Mishnah [pl. *Mishnayos*]: the definitive statements of the Oral Law

Mitzraim: Egypt

mitzvah [pl. *mitzvos*]: commandment

motzaei Shabbos: Saturday evening

nachas: pleasure

nachash: serpent

neshamah: soul

netilas yadayim: washing hands

nistar: hidden

nochri: stranger

parnassah: (earning) a living

parshah: Torah portion

pasuk [pl. *p'sukim*]: Scriptural verses

Pesach: Passover

p'shat: the plain meaning

Pirkei Avos: Ethics of the Fathers; *Mishnah* of ethical teachings

Rambam: Rabbi Moshe ben Maimon (1135 - 1204); Maimonides

Ramban: Rabbi Moshe ben Nachman (1194 - 1270); Nachmanides

rebbe: rabbi, teacher

Ribono Shel Olam: Master of the World

Rosh Hashanah: New Year

schmaltz: fat

seder: Passover night ceremony

Sefer HaChinuch: classic work providing insights into the *mitzvos*

seudah shlishis: the third Shabbos meal

Sforno: classic medieval Torah commentator
Shabbos: Sabbath
Shamayim: Heaven
Shavuos: the festival of Weeks
Shechinah: the Divine Presence
Shemoneh Esrei: eighteen-blessing prayer; main prayer of the
  liturgy
shiur [pl. *shiurim*]: lesson (or lecture)
shivah: lit. "seven," seven-day period of mourning
sh'lita: abbrev. for "May he merit long and good days"
Shlomo Hamelech: King Solomon
shofar: ram's horn sounded on Rosh Hashanah
Shulchan Aruch: Code of Jewish Law
simchah: rejoicing
Succos: festival of Booths; Tabernacles
tachlis: purpose
talmid [pl. *talmidim*]: student
talmid chacham: lit. "a wise student"; an individual learned in
  Torah
Talmud: the Oral Law
Tanach: Scripture
tefillin: phylacteries
teshuvah: repentance; return to Torah observance
Torah min hashamayim: Torah from Heaven
Tosafos: group of medieval commentators on the Talmud
tzaddik [pl. *tzaddikim*]: righteous person
tznius: modesty
Vilna Gaon: Rabbi Eliyahu ben Shlomo Zalman of Vilna
  (1720-1797)
Yaakov Avinu: our father Jacob
yeshiva [pl. *yeshivos*]: academy of Torah learning
Yiddishkeit: Judaism
Yitzchak Avinu: our father Isaac
yom: day
zt"l: zecher tzaddik livrachah — of blessed memory

This volume is part of
THE ARTSCROLLSERIES®
an ongoing project of
translations, commentaries and expositions
on Scripture, Mishnah, Talmud, Halachah,
liturgy, history, the classic Rabbinic writings,
biographies, and thought.

For a brochure of current publications
visit your local Hebrew bookseller
or contact the publisher:

Mesorah Publications, ltd.
4401 Second Avenue
Brooklyn, New York 11232
(718) 921-9000